THE ANTI-INFLAMMATORY DIET PLAN

Your Guide to Beating Inflammation and Pain for Optimal Health, FAST! Includes a Month of Delicious Recipes to Protect your Family from Disease and Allergies

Table of Contents

- Part I: Gluten and Disease
- Chapter One: What is Inflammation?
  -
    - Inflammation and Chronic Disease
    - Understanding the Root of Inflammation and Coeliac Disease
- Chapter Two: Chronic Disease, Pain, and Gluten:
  - Heart Disease and Hypertension
  - Inflammation and Type-II Diabetes
  - Chronic Pain and Insomnia
- Chapter Three: Allergies and Gluten
  - How is Inflammation Connected to Allergy?
  - What is Histamine?
  - Identifying Hives
  - Common Symptoms of Food Allergies
  - Food Allergies in Adults versus Children
  - Additional Causes and Effects of Excessive and Chronic Release of Histamine
  - The Immune System, Allergies, and Stress
  - The Harm of Chronic Use of Anti-Inflammatory Medication
  - Lists of Common Side Effects of Antihistamine Drugs
  - Our Daughter's Story
- Chapter Four: Allergies, Infection, and Food
  - Infection
  - Lists of Common Infections
  - Foods that need to be avoided: "Is this Gluten Free?
  - What is a Gluten Free Diet?
  - Vanessa's Story
- Part II: The Heart of the Matter – Gluten Free Living
- Chapter Five: Nutritional Necessities
  - The Importance of Balanced Diet in Many Inflammatory Conditions
  - Difference between True Hunger and Cravings
  - Know How to Keep Track of your Food Intake
- Why Anti-Inflammatory Diets?
- Can a Diet Really Affect Inflammation?
  - Anti-Inflammatory Diet Principles

- Chapter Six: The Anti-Inflammation Diet
  - Lifestyle Alert: Gluten Free
  - Protein
  - 3 Types of Fats
  - How you Can Prevent Omega-6 Fats from Promoting Inflammation (Tips)
  - Lists of Foods that Help Decrease Inflammation
- Chapter Seven: Enhancing the Quality of Mealtimes
  - Anti-Inflammatory Cooking: A Gluten Free (or Low Gluten Diet)
  - The Anti-Inflammation Diet in Summary (Gluten Free Version)
  - Fast and Easy Gluten Free Recipes
  - A Four Week Meal Plan
- Chapter Eight: Foods and Substitution
  - Sample Gluten Free List – Shopping
  - Modifying Recipes for an Anti-Inflammatory Gluten-Free Diet
  - Lists of Items to be kept on Hand Always
- Chapter Nine: Simplified and Effective Dietary Plan
  - Patients/Members of the family who are suffering from heart disease, arthritis, dementia, and allergies.
- Chapter Ten: Anti-inflammation Recipes & Meal Planning
  - Conclusion "A Healthy Future"
- 53 Delicious Anti-Inflammation Recipes to Keep Your Family Healthy
- BREAK FAST
  - 1. 10-minute Blueberry Oatmeal
  - 2. Breakfast Egg Scramble
  - 3. Blueberry Buckwheat Pancakes
  - 4. Gluten Free Banana Bread
  - 5. Gluten Free Almond-Raspberry Danish Tartlets
  - 6. Breakfast Gluten-free Brownies
  - 7. Spinach and Berries Smoothie
  - 8. Quick Scrambled Egg N' Mushrooms
  - 9. Gluten-free Sugar-free Granola
  - 10. No-Bake Carob Mousse Cake
  - 11. Summer Fresh Fruit Salad
  - 12. Avocado Omelet
  - 13. Flax-Almond Porridge
  - 14. Banana and Blueberry French Toast
  - 15. Pan Fried Halibut with Cilantro Tartar Sauce

- LUNCH
  - 1. Gluten-Free Cream of Mushroom Soup
  - 2. Hot Summer Chili
  - 3. Salmon Egg Salad
  - 4. Fruity Chicken Salad
  - 5. BLT Salad
  - 6. Cedar Planked Salmon Fillets
  - 7. Chicken Fruit Spinach Salad
  - 8. Thai Chicken Noodle Soup
  - 9. Gluten-Free Pepperoni Pizza
  - 10. Quick N' Easy Gluten Free Chicken Stir Fry
  - 11. Easy Baked Tilapia
  - 12. Gluten-Free, Dairy-Free Cherry Turkey Lettuce Wraps
  - 13. Gluten Free Chicken Piccata
  - 14. Pork Tenderloin in Cranberry-Spinach Salad
  - 15. Dijonnaise Tuna Salad on a Bed of Lettuce
- DINNER
  - 1. Gluten free Teriyaki Salmon
  - 2. Honey Mustard Grilled Pork Chops
  - 3. Beef Stuffed Cabbage
  - 4. Raw Veggie Nuts and Seeds Salad
  - 5. Parmigiano Beef Meatballs
  - 6. Grilled Rosemary Lime Swordfish
  - 7. Gluten-free Grilled Pineapple Burgers
  - 8. Spinach N' Mushroom Stuffed Chicken
  - 9. Grilled Tilapia with Black Bean Mango Salsa
  - 10. Grilled Lemon N' Lime Cod Fillets
  - 11. Gluten-free Beef and Broccoli Stir-fry
  - 12. Lemon and Herb Crusted Salmon Fillets
  - 13. Spicy Almond Fish Sticks with Garlic Lime Tartar Sauce
  - 14. Honey-Mustard Lemon Marinated Chicken
  - 15. Roasted Pork Tenderloin with Blueberry Sauce
- DESSERTS and SNACKS
  - 1. Carob Chip Cookies
  - 2. Gluten Free Almond Butter and Banana Sandwiches
  - 3. Citrus Berry Parfait
  - 4. Gluten-Free Chocolate Cupcakes
  - 5. Garbanzo Bean Chocolate Cake

- o 6. Poached Pears and Vanilla Ice Cream with Chocolate-Mango Sauce
- o 7. Almond-stuffed Baked Apples with Almond Whipped Cream
- o 8. Berry Medley Walnut Parfait with Coconut Vanilla Ice Cream
- One Last Thing...

Disclaimer

While all attempts have been made to provide effective, verifiable information in this Book, neither the Author nor Publisher assumes any responsibility for errors, inaccuracies, or omissions. Any slights of people or organizations are unintentional.

This Book is not a source of medical information, and it should not be regarded as such. This publication is designed to provide accurate and authoritative information in regard to the subject matter covered. It is sold with the understanding that the publisher is not engaged in rendering a medical service. As with any medical advice, the reader is strongly encouraged to seek professional medical advice before taking action.

Part I: Gluten and Disease

Chapter One: What is Inflammation?

Inflammation and Chronic Disease

"Some days I was so tired I didn't have the energy to get out of bed! The thought of getting dressed was almost more than I could handle!" Cindy D. Aged 33

Inflammation

Let's get right to the heart of the matter. Inflammation is now considered to be a 'silent killer'. We all know that inflammation is your body's way of responding to injury. Whether you fall and scrape your knee, fight a bad head cold, or come out in hives (as our daughter did), the resulting inflammation is your body's way of combating the attack to the system.

Inflammation of any type is like a 'Band-Aid'. Basically, it is the body's way of protecting itself from any assault. It serves a useful purpose as a way of repairing itself from the damage that bacteria, fungus, virus, injury, and toxins can cause. Inflammation is a process that allows our body to heal.

Whenever any part of our body is damaged, our system immediately engages and starts to fight the enemy. Most of the time, the assault is so minor (acute) that we aren't even aware our body is in an attack mode. As soon as the threat leaves, our system returns to its normal state.

However, when our bodies are required to fight off an assault over an extended period of time, the condition becomes chronic. After a while, the inflammatory reaction fails to cease on its own. This causes stress to the body, ultimately resulting in a weakened state of health.

Chronic Disease

When the immune system is continuously called into action, the condition becomes chronic and can lead to several chronic ailments. Alzheimer's disease, heart disease, diabetes, cancer and allergies can all be linked to chronic inflammation. For this reason, it has been referred to as the 'silent killer'. In my daughter's case, as I will illustrate later in this book, my wife and I were completely unaware of the effect gluten had on her body!

In my case, I was experiencing the result of chronic inflammation to my joints, almost to the point where I believed that I might have to give up tennis! As I looked more deeply into the area of inflammation and chronic disease, I learned that inflammatory conditions take away energy and an overall feeling of well-being. The wear-and-tear of over stressing the immune system can cause chronic fatigue, aches and pains, and a variety of other inflammatory problems.

Understanding the Root of Inflammation and Coeliac Disease

"What causes inflammation and gluten related coeliac disease?" Candace M. (Age 28)
Digestion and Inflammation

To understand how food and allergies are related to inflammation, it helps to understand how digestion occurs in the gastrointestinal tract. Every time we eat, the food is first ground up by our teeth. It then travels down the esophagus to the stomach and is further broken down, by enzymes and acids, into a soft paste-like substance. The food then travels into the small intestines where the nutrients are absorbed. The remainder of the digested food travels into the large intestines and the most of the last remnants of salt and water are absorbed before the waste is eliminated by the body. This process can take between 24 and 72 hours depending on the general health of the intestines.

This description is very basic, and the entire process is far more involved than what I've described here. The point is that when everything is working in a healthy manner, proteins are broken into single amino acids and fats are metabolized into fatty acids, and carbohydrates are broken up into simple sugars. When everything is in good working order, these nutrients are properly absorbed, without causing an allergic reaction. However, if the cells lining the intestinal tract are hypersensitive, there may be a resulting imbalance and a strong possibility that the food cannot be properly digested.

Food Allergies and Coeliac Disease

As I've mentioned, this is an overly simplified explanation. However, the point that I want to stress is that there is a direct link between food allergies (particularly in this case to gluten) and many health conditions like asthma, arthritis, eczema, and heart diseases. Since more than 70% of the cells that support the immune system are located in the lining of the digestive tract, it isn't surprising that when food isn't right for your needs, your system will be thrown into a mode of attack. While many foods are healthy, foods that you are allergic to are responded to like toxins, harmful invaders. Blood flow increases and the intestines become inflamed.

Coeliac disease (or celiac disease) is one of the conditions that can result from the body's inability to stop the inflammation process in the digestive tract. The resulting pain and fatigue are symptoms of the small intestine's difficulty in absorbing proper nutrition. When this happens they react to certain food particles as foreign substances. One of the primary causes for the disease is gluten sensitivity or, in other words, gluten intolerance that can often be remedied with a gluten free celiac diet.

Chapter Two: Chronic Disease, Pain, and Gluten:

Heart Disease and Hypertension
"The greatest wealth is health." Virgil

I use the term heart disease broadly to include other conditions such as stroke, heart attack, atherosclerosis, and high blood pressure. While there are several risk factors associated with heart disease, inflammation is known to be one of them. Damage to the microscopic cells results from microscopic tissue damage. As mentioned earlier, low-grade inflammation that occurs over a period of time is known to increase the risk of disease to the heart. Anything that disturbs the balance of the vascular (heart) cells can potentially increase the risk of heart disease.

Epithelial cells that line the blood vessels control the flow of hormones, nutrients, and immune facilitators that help to regulate blood flow and proper functioning of the circulatory system and regulate blood pressure. The cells that help support the immune system help to protect the delicate tissues from attacks. Inflammation that is chronic is the most frequent offense to proper cardiovascular function.

Inflammation and Hypertension

When tissue is injured or exposed to toxic substances, the body reacts to the assault with inflammation. The epithelial cells respond by producing molecules that are known to increase the risk of heart disease. Clotting and coagulation, abnormal bleeding, and vascular regulators can all be affected. Nitric oxide (NO), one of the tone regulators, helps to regulate blood pressure. Elevated blood sugar levels, over a period of time, decreases the level of NO and increasing the blood pressure, resulting in hypertension.

Hypertension can cause cells to lose elasticity. When this happens, lesions can form along the blood vessels. Ultimately, the cells can weaken and result in an aneurysm. Aneurysms can then burst and cause instantaneous death!

The good news is that by avoiding unhealthy foods it is possible to reduce inflammation to the circulatory system and help take the stress off of the heart and other bodily systems.

Inflammation and Type-II Diabetes

Low-level chronic inflammation is considered to be another significant risk-factor related to Type-II diabetes. Research documents that diets that are loaded with foods that cause inflammation, such as sugar, and highly processed grains and meats may result in the increased likelihood for developing Type-II diabetes. Medical researchers have been aware of this potential risk for several years.

Chronic Pain and Insomnia

Many types of chronic pain, like fibromyalgia, can be the result of inflammation. Even though fibromyalgia doesn't fall under the category of inflammatory disease, one of the symptoms of the illness is inflammation. For patients suffering from fibromyalgia, disrupted sleep patterns contributes to the delay in getting well. We know that the immune system works 24/7 cleansing our system and making repairs, especially when we sleep. If sleep is disturbed, as it is for many people who suffer from fibromyalgia, this cleansing/repair process is not able to work at an optimal level.

Why Gluten Free?

When this impairment of the cleansing/repair process occurs, cells and tissues suffer from prolonged inflammation because of the inadequate cleaning within the system. Waste products begin to accumulate. For many people who suffer from this condition, serotonin levels are affected. This change in level can negatively impact mood, sleep, new tissue growth, and the metabolism of carbohydrates, necessary for renewed energy throughout the day. Individuals with fibromyalgia must have a healthy digestive system.

A healthy gluten free diet may counter this negative cycle and help reduce the unpleasant gluten symptoms of the illness by decreasing inflammation.

When the gastrointestinal system is functioning adequately, inflammation is reduced, and serotonin secretions improve. This can elevate a person's mood and allow for quality sleep. The positive result is that the immune-system's ability to cleanse and repair the body during the night is restored. The gluten free diet plan is recognized by many health providers as an effective way to help eliminate chronic pain and insomnia.

Gluten is a combination of plant proteins found in many grains and other food products. Gluten-free diets are designed to omit all types of food that contain large amounts of gluten. Gluten can be found in wheat, barley, rye, triticale, kamut, oats and spelt. Interestingly, rice and corn include gluten but in a form that doesn't trigger celiac disease, so are considered gluten free. While all grains contain some form of gluten. Gluten-free generally means foods that do not contain rye, barley, and wheat.

Chapter Three: Allergies and Gluten

"At first my skin felt dry and irritated. Within a couple of days, my skin was red and itchy. When I scratched my hands, puffy bumps began to rise along my arms. These welts grew larger at an alarming rate. I did not understand why this was happening." Julie (Aged 40)

How is Inflammation Connected to Allergy?

In general, allergies result when the immune system (over) reacts to foreign substances. A healthy immune system is ready to protect the body from the invasion of any unwanted agent into your system. When successful, your immune system protects your system from infection and disease.

However, because the immune system is not always able to differentiate between good, neutral, and harmful invaders it tends to over-react. This hyperactive immunity can cause your body to go into a tail-spin and react to even 'harmless visitors' with prolonged inflammation. These 'visitors' are referred to as allergens. Resulting inflammation may occur suddenly or persist, causing mild to severe allergic reactions.

What is Histamine?

When a person has an allergy, the body produces antibodies as a way to safeguard itself from intrusion. As a response, countless antibodies attach to the surface of the cells within bodily tissue. There they wait for the next attack by an allergen that the body has identified as a potential threat. While on guard, they collect assorted chemicals from blood as it circulates through the system, resulting in inflammation.

When another assault takes place, the allergen is bound by specific antibodies and a chemical is released. Histamine, one of these specially designed chemicals contributes to the allergic response set up within the body. Histamine is associated with sneezing, runny noses, itching, and many of the other discomforts associated with allergic reactions.

Anti-allergy medications, referred to as antihistamines, are designed to prevent the histamines from binding to 'receptors'. Allergic reactions have two phases. There is an early phase, caused when the chemicals are released that can happen immediately after exposure to an allergen. A late phase reaction, occurring when inflammatory cells are brought in for back-up, can occur many hours after exposure. Allergic reactions may cause hives on the skin's surface. Usually hives appear on the arms, legs, and torso, but they may occur on other parts of the body as well. A severe allergic reaction, such as the one our daughter experienced, can cause swelling within the mouth, tongue, and throat.

Identifying Hives

Typical hives appear on the surface of the skin as raised, reddish bumps (welts). Many times they are accompanied by itching and general discomfort, such as stinging or burning. They range in size anywhere from between a fraction of an inch to the size of a small dish. The entire area of skin may become swollen and inflamed. The skin around the eyes may swell, and the lips may become swollen. As mentioned earlier, hives may appear suddenly or over a period of time. Although welts are a common occurrence they are not always a symptom of an allergic reaction.

When a person does break out in hives, they usually appear on one part of the body then spread rather rapidly to other parts of the body. It's not unusual for the welts to grow larger and merge with other hives (or welts). Occasionally these welts can expand over very large surfaces of the skin. The spreading of the hives can cause sensations like shivering, burning, and intense itching. The welts may appear and disappear, then reappear over the course a few minutes or several days. Hives are associated with allergic reactions to many types of allergens, including those associated with food allergies.

Common Symptoms of Food Allergies

Hives are one of the many visible signs of a food allergy. I've learned through my research that certain foods may trigger a variety of problems. As we have already seen, there is a connection between inflammation and several illnesses, diseases, and food allergies, many of which are related to gluten.

As we have just learned, there are many substances that can prompt an allergic reaction. What I found most alarming was the direct connection between certain foods, particularly those containing gluten (the protein in wheat) and food allergies! It's important to note that gluten and milk cause two of the most common food allergies which emphasize the advantages of a gluten free dairy free diet!

Allow me to elaborate. A food allergy is caused by the immune-system's response to certain proteins found in food. As in other types of allergic reactions, certain foods can cause the release of histamine. A variety of symptoms can result, from a runny nose, and sneezing, to hives, stomach cramps, and diarrhea, to anaphylaxis (an extremely serious condition that occurs rapidly occasionally resulting in death).

And if that's not alarming enough, this reaction could potentially happen at any time. Anyone who has an allergic reaction may have anywhere between a very minor to a major reaction (*as my daughter did*). Whenever the offending food is consumed, certain antibodies may be activated that can bind with the food particles and stimulate an autoimmune-inflammatory reaction. As we have learned, inflammation of any type can interfere with the body's ability to heal and metabolize food properly. Additionally, these food allergens are usually not properly digested and build up in the liver, kidneys, and all of the organs that are associated with detox within the body. After eliminating glutens from their diet, many people no longer experience allergic reactions to food. The common symptoms include those that we have already identified. The following chart shows the many symptoms and signs of food allergies.

Common Symptoms of Food Allergy (Table)

COMMON SYMPTOMS OF FOOD ALLERGIES		Subjective SYMPTOMS	SIGNS
Skin Conditions	Skin	Itching	Skin Redness/Hives Eczema, Swelling (usually on the face)
	Mouth and Eyes	Itching, Numbness	Edema, Redness and Tearing
GASTROINTESTINAL		Nausea, Pain	Vomiting, Diarrhea, Abdominal Pain
RESPIRATORY	Nose/Larynx/Throat/ Lungs	Itching/ Dry/Tightness Shortness of Breath Chest Pain/Tightness	Swelling, Hoarseness, Wheezing, Cough, Respiratory Distress

HEART AND CARDIOVASCULAR		Chest Pain/ Tightness/Feeling Dizziness/Faintness	Fainting, Loss of Consciousness Hypotension or shock (low blood pressure), Abnormal Heart Beat
OTHER		Feeling of Impending Disaster	Uterine Contractions (women)

However, many signs are not quite so obvious. It took me a long time to make the connection between my painful joints and the large amounts of gluten that I was consuming! (I also want to point out adults and children don't always react to food allergens in the same way.)

Food Allergies in Adults versus Children

When very young children (or babies) experience food allergies, they may be the result of prenatal or hereditary factors. Allergies may also be the result of intestinal cell damage that can occur if a child is fed formula, rather than breast milk, or solid baby food at too early an age. This damage often occurs if the intestines are still too immature to handle the foods.

When food allergies develop later on in a person's life, the allergy is generally the result of chemical or physical damage within the cells of the intestines. For example, food poisoning may cause permanent intestinal damage, when the toxins cannot be properly handled and eliminated. When this happens, an auto-immune response can be activated that causes inflammation within the intestines and throughout the entire body. The vulnerable parts of the body usually suffer the most. When damage takes place over time, inflammation (tissue and organ damage) may result in an imbalance that becomes chronic. For this reason, repairing the damage to tissue and organs begins with paying attention to food intake and proper digestion. Along with allergies, the serious health issues previously mentioned: arthritis, heart disease, skin problems, and asthma often can be remedied, at least in part, by changing our diet and focusing on the foods that can be properly digested.

The longer food allergies persist, the greater the damaged caused. The best measure is to take a serious look at the possibility of food allergies and gluten intolerance within your family, and start making healthy changes as soon as possible in order to avoid illness, disease, allergies and infection.

Additional Causes and Effects of Excessive and Chronic Release of Histamine

As we've already learned, histamine is a chemical within our bodies at all times. It is created and stored within specialized cells and helps the immune system in defending the body against foreign infection and unwelcomed substances. In addition, histamine also acts as one of the brain's 'messengers' and aides in releasing gastric-acid to facilitate digestion within the stomach. Research has demonstrated that there are many people who are hypersensitive. This hypersensitivity can result in excessive amounts of histamine when it is exposed to allergens in the environment or in the foods that are consumed. Elevated levels of histamine can cause a variety of reactions and symptoms, ranging from mild distress to full blown allergic reactions.

High levels of histamine may trigger itching on one side of the body or both. The itching is caused when other types of inflammation and irritations are triggered by excessively high levels of histamine.

Likewise, large amounts of histamine can cause watery, itchy red eyes, nasal congestion, runny noses, sneezing, irritation to the eyes and ears, and post nasal drip. This type of reaction is usually in response to airborne allergens.

Asthmatic reactions can also occur when there are excessive histamine levels in the bloodstream. This potentially serious and chronic condition takes place when there are increased mucous secretions in the respiratory system. Wheezing, difficulty with breathing and tightness of the chest are common symptoms.

Over production of histamines can cause swelling in deep tissue, resulting in swelling of the digestive tract, throat, mouth, and restrict breathing, sometimes fatally. A very severe reaction to high levels of histamine can cause Anaphylaxis.

Various symptoms of this potentially life threatening condition may include a sudden dip in blood pressure, abdominal pain, diarrhea, swollen and reddened skin, nausea, vomiting, nasal congestion, coughing, wheezing, difficulty breathing, dizziness and fainting.

The Immune System, Allergies, and Stress

The effect of stress on our system can cause several adverse reactions. Our systems have the built in ability to handle stress. Stress causes a sudden increase in energy, brought about by stimulation by the stress hormone, cortisol. In our highly stressful world, this response can be triggered at any time, even while sitting in rush hour traffic. The sudden burst of energy allows for 'fight or flight', yet most of the time we don't have the opportunity to use this increased energy. Because we have no way to use the blood sugar, we are often left with constantly elevated levels of cortisol. This prolonged elevation can weaken the immune system, increase the likelihood of allergic reactions, inflammation, and increase the risk of many stress related health problems.

The Harm of Chronic Use of Anti-Inflammatory Medication
Over use of any medication to counteract inflammatory reactions carries certain risks. In the case of anti-inflammatories, the risks include cardiovascular problems, erectile dysfunction, gastrointestinal problems, inflammatory bowel disease, renal difficulties, and difficulties during pregnancy, possible drug interactions, to name a few!

Due to the increased use of anti-inflammatories the negative effects have become progressively worse. The primary adverse reactions include gastrointestinal and renal damage. The side-effects can include ulcers, gastrointestinal bleeding, and the risk of death.

Lists of Common Side Effects of Antihistamine Drugs
There are several side effects related to antihistamine drugs. Some of these side effects are listed in the chart below.

Lists of Common Side Effects of Antihistamine Drugs
Anxiety
Drowsiness
Dry Mouth
Heart Palpitations
Problems with Constipation
Problems with Urination

Chapter Four: Allergies, Infection, and Food

"I'd been eating whole wheat bread because I thought it was healthier. I couldn't believe it when I found out I was allergic to wheat!" Sarah Jo (Age 29)

More about Food Allergies

As we can see, a definite pattern is emerging. All of our organs must work together to keep us alive. The digestive system's purpose is to process the food we eat, to give us energy, and allow for optimal health. After the food has been ingested, it is broken down, nutrients are absorbed into our system, and waste products are eliminated. The healthier the food choices, the more effective and beneficial the results!

For this reason, following a nutritional, well balanced diet can help us avoid many of the health problems previously discussed and avoid the accumulated waste in the digestive tract. A healthy diet helps to increase energy levels and a sense of well-being.

Along with the foods that we consume, we are constantly exposed to toxins in our environment. Without intending to, we inadvertently consume growth hormones in food, minute amounts of antibiotics, pesticides and other chemicals. Our system is working overtime in order to eliminate the unwanted elements while digesting the healthy nutrients. The kidneys and liver worked together to metabolize what we consume. Although highly efficient, this process is never totally effective. Every one of us has a unique way of processing food and responding to the environment. The most effective way to find a healthy balance is to become informed and to tune into your individual needs. Not only will you look and feel better, you will be likely to have far more energy and a much greater ability to ward off disease and infection!

Infection

As we've learned, poor health and allergies tax our body in many different ways. Another factor that compromises the immune system is infection. No matter how careful we are to avoid exposure to infection, there are viruses, parasites, and yeasts that reside within our own bodies at all times. Although they are there, they don't necessarily pose a threat. However, when the immune system is compromised, we become far more susceptible to illness.

When we become ill, often our first reaction is to treat the ailment with an antibiotic. Although antibiotics can serve a useful purpose, they are not always the best solution. While antibiotics may kill harmful bacteria, they also kill the beneficial bacteria within our body, thus damaging intestinal tissue. Extensive research supports a strong connection between inflammation, disease, and infection, particularly those related to the digestive system.

Lists of Common Infections

I think it is helpful to include a list of some of the most common types of infections and ailments that adults and children face today. While the lists are not in any way complete, I believe that they help to illustrate the very real health threats that we face every day.

The following is a list of some of the most common infections and health concerns diagnosed in children, young adults, and older adults:

Common Infections in Children and Young Adults
Chicken Pox
Croup
Immune System Problems
Ear Infections
Head Lice
MRSA
Pneumonia
Ringworm
Respiratory Syncytial Virus (RSV)
Salmonella
Scabies
Sexually Transmitted Diseases (STDs)
Sore Throats
West Nile Virus Update
Cold and Flu
Whooping Cough

Common Infections in Older Adults
Bacterial Pneumonia
Herpes Zoster (also known as shingles)

Influenza
Urinary tract infections (UTI)

Now that we better understand the types of ailments and infections that our families are susceptible to, it is helpful to include a chart with some of the top foods that help fight infection.

(Some of the) Top Five Foods that Fight Infections
Beta-carotene and Vitamin A: (i.e. carrots, kale, spinach, squash)
Vitamin C: (natures remedy for the body)
Garlic Cloves
Probiotics: (found in some dairy products such as yogurt)
Foods that contain Zinc

Foods that need to be avoided: "Is this Gluten Free?

The most important step in adopting a gluten free diet is becoming aware of what you are putting into your body. As I mentioned earlier, my wife and I believed that we were health conscious, but over the course of several years we had started to rely more and more heavily on processed foods that were easy and quick to prepare. Our first step was to pay closer attention to what we were feeding our family. In addition to following the gluten free plan, that I will go into in more detail in Part II, we started looking for fresh foods that were locally and organically grown. We wanted to buy foods that hadn't spent days traveling to the store! We knew that the fresher the vegetables and fruit, the more beneficial they were likely to be. Food that is heavily processed tends to contain more toxic substances and fewer energy producing nutrients. We realized that the difficulty is to determine what ingredients have gone into the processing of food; the more likely it is to be unhealthy.

Seasonal foods tend to be the healthiest. Boxed, canned, and dehydrated foods that have a 'long shelf life' are loaded with additives, color, and preservatives and generally contain fewer nutrients than their fresh counterparts.

While supplements can replace some of our nutritional needs, whole foods are the only real source for the healthy proteins, carbohydrates and beneficial fats that our body needs. Consuming processed foods over the course of several days will leave us feeling depleted and listless.

The list below is a partial list that includes the types of foods that are known to cause food allergies, as well as a list of foods containing gluten.

Lists of Foods that Need to be Avoided	Foods with Gluten to be Avoided
Artificial Additives	See Additive List Below***
Sweeteners and Artificial Sweeteners and Sugar (Candy)	***
Old and Moldy Fruit	
Alcoholic Beverages	Malt
Carbonated Beverages and Soft drinks	***
Smoked and Cured Commercial Meats	***
Foods Containing Vinegar and White Vinegar	
Products with Processed Oil	***
Gluten Grains	Wheat, Barley, Rye, Oats
Dairy	
Regular Black Tea and Coffee	
Yeast	
Rancid Nuts and Seeds and Peanuts	
Processed Soy Products	***
Vegetables from the Nightshade Family	
Corn	

What is a Gluten Free Diet?
Until now, I have emphasized many of the illnesses, diseases, and other health concerns that are

tied to our diet and nutrition. Specifically I would like to turn our focus to those foods containing gluten. Generally, a gluten free diet means eliminating, or avoiding, several grains including wheat, rye, and barley. It's clear that a gluten free diet would rule out most breads, pastries, and pasta. It is not always quite as apparent when we consider the food additives in processed foods. In the chart above I have listed some of the primary sources of gluten. I have also highlighted some of the less obvious sources. As you can see, gluten is often 'hidden' in many food additives.

Some Top Food Additives to Avoid
Flavor Additives: such as butterscotch, caramel, rice malt, brown rice, or rice syrup
Hydrolyzed Vegetable Protein: HVPs that are processed with wheat (gluten)
Malt: obtained from barley (a grain containing gluten)
Modified Food Starch: may contain: potato, corn, tapioca, or wheat

In Part II, I will explain some of the food substitutions that can be made in a gluten-free diet. (I want to add that there is some cross-over between foods that may cause allergies and those that are gluten-free.) Here, I will highlight a few possible gluten free substitutions.

Identify an Allergy-Free (Gluten Free) Diet

Allergy Substitution Chart (Sample Lists)
Gluten Free Grains, Gluten Free Flours, Starch: Corn, Sorghum, Rice
Legume Flours: ChickPeas, Fava Beans, Peanuts, Soy
Nut Flours: Almond, Chestnut, Walnut
Seed Flours: Amaranth, Buckwheat, Flaxseed, Millet, Quinoa
Tuber Starches/Flour: Potato, Sweet Potato, Tapioca

Vanessa's Story:

"Hi, my name is Vanessa. I am a good friend of the author's wife. Lynn and I have worked together as recreational therapists for over ten years. A couple of years ago, I noticed that Lynn seemed to have more energy than ever before. Her complexion was flawless, and she had stopped drinking that second cup of coffee that Lynn always said she needed to keep her energy up.

At that very same time, I was experiencing health problems. At age 38, I had recently given birth to my fourth child and for several months I'd been suffering from reoccurring ear infections *and breaking out in hives. My doctor had put me on an antihistamine and a series of antibiotics. There were only a few types of antibiotics that I was able to take because I was still nursing our daughter. It was against my nature to take any medications, but I wasn't aware of any alternatives. I felt terrible. I was run down, and barely getting any sleep.*

I commented to Lynn that I noticed she was looking unusually healthy while I, on the other hand, was depleted. Even though I craved foods, I was always hungry. I admitted to Lynn that I felt pretty miserable!

Lynn told me about her husband's research, and about the changes that they had made in their family's diet. I listened attentively. At that point, I was willing to try almost anything, as long as it was healthy for my family, our baby, and me. The more I learned, the more excited I became.

I followed the food plan that has included in this book. Now, two years later, I am grateful to say that my entire family is healthy and strong. I have the energy that I need to keep up with our daughter, now two-and-a-half, my husband (an avid downhill skier), and our three teen-aged sons!

Thanks to Lynn (and Mr. Fleischer), I feel better and have more energy than I have had in years! And, I no longer suffer from hives and painful ear infections!" Vanessa (Age 41)

Our family friend made an interesting comment. She stated that she craved food all of the time, yet always felt hungry. If we eat the wrong foods for the wrong reasons we can, in fact, be starving our bodies, even when we 'overeat'. Part II elaborates on our nutritional needs.

Part II: The Heart of the Matter – Gluten Free Living

Chapter Five: Nutritional Necessities

"We are living in a world today where lemonade is made from artificial flavors and furniture polish is made from real lemons." Alfred E. Newman

The Importance of Balanced Diet in Many Inflammatory Conditions

Let's quickly review the primary causes of inflammation in order to understand the significance of a balanced diet. As we have already discussed several of the most common types of inflammation including: infection, allergies, environmental toxins, injury, emotional trauma, nutritional deficiencies and excesses.

Infection: When an infection occurs in the system, it is because a fungus, bacterium, yeast, virus, or another type of parasite assaults the system. The immune system prepares for battle and reacts with an inflammation that is specifically designed to attack the infection.

Allergy: As previously discussed, an allergic reaction occurs when the system over responds to any substance (either harmful or harmless) that may potentially be a threat to the body. This could be anything from a specific food to an insect bite. The body responds with inflammation as a way to defend the body. Reactions may range from mild to severe.

Toxicity and Injury: Inflammation may occur when cells are exposed to chemical or physical irritants. Many toxins (pesticides, tobacco, drugs, asbestos, etc.) may potentially cause injury to bodily tissue. Continual exposure frequently results in inflammation as a way to protect and heal the affected areas. Inflammation is a natural way for the body to heal and repair cells and tissues that have been injured.

Emotional Trauma: Stress and anxiety can have an adverse effect on the body. Mental distress has a direct link with a person's physiology. When an individual undergoes emotional stress elevated levels of cortisone and adrenaline are released and can result in an imbalance and inflammation. Aging has a tendency to make the situation worse. The overload is often more than the body is prepared to handle. When a person is in good health, toxins are more readily flushed from the system.

Nutritional Deficiency and Nutritional Excess: Hormone imbalances, taxed immune system, and inflammation are frequently tied to imbalances in nutrition. Nutritional deficiencies such as a lack of the proper protein fats, carbohydrates, vitamins and minerals may leave the system lacking in the nutrients necessary for cell and tissue repair. Conversely, excessive amounts of certain foods can lead to a nutritional imbalance that can stress the bodily tissues and organs.

As you can see, many factors come into play: mental health, exercise, environmental conditions, lifestyle factors, along with a genetic predisposition and diet. When we make a point of reducing our family's exposure to toxins, become more aware of how we treat our body, and watch what we eat, we give ourselves an increased ability to handle potentially threatening conditions. In Part II of this book, we will focus on the importance of combating inflammation through an understanding of our dietary needs and the gluten free diet.

Difference between True Hunger and Cravings

Hunger is a built in device that allows us to tune into our body's unique nutritional needs. When a person experiences food cravings generally there may be a nutritional deficiency. A craving for salty foods, for example, could indicate a salt deficiency. However, many food cravings have an emotional component; often when people are dieting and attempting to eliminate a particular type they will experience cravings for that food.

Say, for example, you have been in the habit of eating a bag of chips while sitting at the computer in the evening. If you should decide to cut that activity out of your routine, you're likely to go through a period where you crave the chips. A good way to determine if you are experiencing genuine hunger or a craving is to imagine replacing the chips with another type of food, say an apple...if the idea of the apple satisfies the need then more than likely what you are experiencing is true hunger. If only chips will do...you're most likely experiencing a food craving. (Sometimes there is an underlying condition that may require a medical evaluation.)

When a person eats for the right reasons they are usually only eating when they are truly hungry and will stop eating when they are satisfied, and not overly full. Generally, a satisfying diet will include nutritious food while not ruling out foods that are especially enjoyable. However, when a person becomes ruled by food cravings, there is a tendency to gain weight, overeat, and suffer nutritionally.

Below is a chart that distinguishes between signs of genuine hunger/cravings and emotional food cravings. Keep in mind that hunger effects people in different ways.

Genuine Food Cravings	Emotional Food Cravings
Physiologically Hungry	Not Physiologically Hungry
Craving Continue and Can't be 'Waited Out'	It Goes Away and Can be 'Waited Out'
Cravings Intensify as Time Passes	Cravings Do Not Intensify; the Emotion Does
Nothing Will do but the Craved Food.	The Craving Can be Replaced With Something Else

Know How to Keep Track of your Food Intake

The simplest way to stay in tune with your body is by keeping a food journal. A food journal allows you to keep track of your eating habits. You can record how you feel prior to eating, while eating, and after eating. Keep track of how hungry you are at various stages throughout the day. By getting in touch with triggers and patterns, you'll soon be able to recognize and avoid giving in to emotional cravings. If emotions get the best of you, you may be able to replace that bag of chips with sensible, gluten free snacks. (I have included a sample journal page at the end of this section.)

Emotions and eating patterns are closely linked. Your journal will help to make connections between emotions and eating habits. With practice, you can replace eating foods that cause inflammation with gluten free foods that help to promote better health. Gluten free recipes and meal plans, included in this book, will provide healthy alternatives. As you tune into your true nutritional needs, you are likely to feel healthier in every way.

Another suggestion is to have a friend or relative make the changes with you. In my case, my wife and I began following a gluten free program together. When the contents of our cupboards and refrigerator began to change we made each decision together. When one of us felt the need for an unhealthy snack, the other was there to suggest healthy alternatives.

At first it was rather slow going, but as partners we became a united front and in turn modeled healthy changes and behaviors for our children! Even though my wife and I keep very busy schedules we shop and cook together, at least once a week. We use this time to look for specials and try out new gluten free recipes.

Why Anti-Inflammatory Diets?

As we can see our diet is a complex set of factors. Our entire system is affected by our attitude about food as well as by the food itself. The nutrients that we take in impact every organ in our body and have a strong bearing on our immune system. The immune system is made up of a complicated series of parts. All of the systems have to be properly cared for. If they are not, the entire process can be thrown off balance. When the immune system is not in check, we become much more susceptible to illness and a variety of health problems. An inadequate immune system is less able to fight off the invasion of a variety of unwanted attackers.

Such an imbalance, where unwanted invasion remains unchecked, can lead to chronic inflammation and disease as well as other autoimmune reactions.

An anti-Inflammation diet helps to prevent such an imbalance and sets up the system for healing and optimal health. Research and firsthand experience have demonstrated many advantages to the body that an anti-inflammation diet provides. The anti-inflammatory diet is beneficial in that it helps avoid many of the foods that set up allergic reactions within the body. It also prevents many unwanted agents from finding their way into our systems. Harmful chemicals, hormones, and antibiotic deposits are warded off by a healthy immune system. An anti-inflammatory diet is beneficial in that it includes whole, natural foods. Foods that are highly processed are eliminated or kept to a minimum. While healthy foods, high in beneficial nutrients, are added to our system.

An anti-inflammation diet facilitates digestion and causes less damage to the body. A circulatory/digestive system that receives a proper balance of nutrients does not have to process difficult to digest foods. It is freed up to metabolize foods that ensure optimal health.

Can a Diet Really Affect Inflammation?

After conducting extensive research, I firmly believe that diet affects inflammation. The diet program that I am presenting in this book is a combination of many of the elements found in a gluten free diet coupled with an anti-inflammatory diet. Just a reminder, every person responds to foods in a different way. I do believe that incorporating some or all of these principles into one's diet can help with positive and lasting health benefits.

As we shall see, eliminating gluten from ones diet (especially in the form of highly processed white flour and sugar) will immediately help to improve overall health. Additionally, eliminating highly processed meats (many of which contain gluten as an additive), allows the system to work smoothly. My family and I noticed immediate improvements in our overall health. However, for some individuals results may occur more gradually. If you have consulted your physician as a result of a chronic disease, switching to an anti-inflammatory/gluten free diet may begin to pave the way for improved health.

An anti-inflammatory diet can provide several health benefits. This book gives suggestions for eliminating and reintroducing the foods that may be culprits in your daily diet. By keeping a daily food journal and adhering to these practices, my hope is that you will also experience many of the health benefits that my family has gained. The following chapters will elaborate on many of the practical anti-inflammatory and gluten free diet principles that you can incorporate into your daily diet/health routine.

Anti-Inflammatory Diet Principles

Our health is affected by the choices we make now, choices that can potentially impact us in years to come. As our children grow, their bodily systems are developing in countless ways. Their brain, immune, and sensitive nervous system continues to develop into young adulthood. The best way to enhance this process is through proper nutrition and lifestyle choices. The principles of the anti-inflammatory and gluten free diet are built on a foundation that calls for reducing exposure to toxic substances while basing a daily diet on proper nutrition. The earlier we promote the principles of a healthy lifestyle, the more likely we are to live vigorous lives and avoid chronic illness in the future.

In addition to a focus on a healthy life, it is my strong belief that we must foster emotional health in our children. As healthy adults, we show our children our love and belief in them through our actions and our words. I want to point out that mild illnesses in children often helps to build a stronger immune system. Just as our children develop, their ability to ward off infection is also increasing. Their immune system is "practicing" and developing. If we attempt to suppress the immune system through the use of unnecessary suppressants, we are influencing the body's natural ability to ward off potential threats. We need to strive to set up a natural balance, one that is assisted *by a healthy diet that naturally aides the body's immunities.*

Chapter Six: The Anti-Inflammation Diet

"Everything that can be counted does not necessarily count; everything that counts cannot necessarily be counted." - Albert Einstein

Lifestyle Alert: Gluten Free
Living gluten-free changes almost every aspect of our life. We needed to rethink not only the foods that we were eating, we had to reevaluate the way in which we shopped, selected recipes, and prepared our family's meals. In the next few chapters, I have provided a four week meal plan, shopping guides, and recipes that will help you along your path to living a gluten-free and anti-inflammatory diet.

If you are one of the countless people who suffer from digestive difficulties, chronic disease, allergies, sleeping problems, skin problems, and mood swings, this "Lifestyle Alert: Gluten Free" diet may be exactly what you are looking for.

Protein
One of the best ways to ensure that you are maintaining the right balance of nutrients and adequate blood sugar levels is by eating the right type of proteins. Many researchers feel that organic protein sources are the most advantageous because they help avoid unwanted exposure to pesticides, hormones, and antibiotics that may be added to meat. Grass fed, organic beef is also recommended in moderation (1-2 portions per week) as well as other organic meats and poultry.

Soy is another acceptable protein source. The best types include tofu and soy milk. Many legumes, nuts, and seeds provide good protein sources. When gluten free grains and legumes are served in combination, they provide a complete protein.

Other excellent protein sources are found in free range eggs and chickens that have developed without the use of antibiotics. The recommended way to prepare eggs is to poach, slow-cook, or boil them in order to avoid damaging the protein. Additionally, avocados are an excellent source for protein as well as being a good source for healthy fat.

3 Types of Fats
The primary types of fat include the monounsaturated (found in olive oils, peanut oils, sesame

seed oils, canola oils and avocados), saturated (beef fat, cheese...connected to cancer, heart disease, other health problems), and polyunsaturated fats (omega-3 fatty acids). Unhealthy fats can increase inflammation causing a series of undesirable reactions. The adage "eat less, move more" also applies to fats. The energy stored in fat is burned while exercising, an overall reduction in fat consumption reduces the number of calories that go into our system, slowing down and preventing unwanted fat storage.

For people with diabetes, eating fatty foods can send the blood sugar level soaring. When the consumption of fats (especially unhealthy fats) is out of balance, our body's response is to defend itself with inflammation.

As blood sugar levels increase, your body has to work extra hard to bring the blood sugar levels back into a normal range. In very simple terms, what this results in is fat storage usually in the stomach area. Studies have shown that individuals who eat food with a 'low glycemic indexes' like whole grains and vegetables, tended to be thinner than those who eat large quantities of white bread, sugary foods, and white potatoes.

Omega-3 Fats are considered to be a 'super-foods', foods that may help lower the risks of the diseases and health problems that we have addressed. A diet high in omega-3 may help lower the risk of heart disease and diabetes. Omega-3 is beneficial in that smaller doses can allow your body to function at an optimal level. Without adequate amounts of omega-3, your body is forced to use omega-6 fats (which we will discuss in more detail).

There are two types of omega-3 fats. One type is found in certain types of fish like salmon, mackerel, and herring. This type of fat is easily metabolized and enriching. The second type is found in certain nuts, seeds, beans, and legumes (i.e. walnuts, soybeans, and flaxseed). This type is beneficial, but is not as effective as the first type because it has to be converted by your system to obtain optimal benefits.

Omega-3s help boost the immune system and decrease inflammation. Since your body depends on a certain amount of fat to run properly, by eating the most beneficial fats you are providing a decided advantage. Some of the best sources for omega-3 are trout, tuna, mackerel, whitefish, halibut, salmon, and sardines. The addition, these foods help boost your immune system and prevent inflammation! Sardines, cod, salmon, and snapper are types of fish known to contain lower doses of mercury, especially those that are 'farmed' and caught in the wild. Additionally, when daily exercise is combined with an adequate intake of omega-3 fats, your body is in a better position to fight the accumulation of body fat.

How you Can Prevent Omega-6 Fats from Promoting Inflammation (Tips)

Most diets are very high in the omega-6 fats and low in omega-3 fats. Research supports that an approximate ratio of 2:1 for omega-6/omega-3 fats may substantially lower inflammation levels.

Additionally, research demonstrates that individuals whose diets include higher ratios of omega-3 fats have lower inflammatory levels.

The majority of omega-6 fats are found in grains, baked products, candy, and snack foods. Where do all these omega-6 fats come from? The majority of omega-6 fats in people's diets come from baked goods, grains, snack foods and candy. Soybean oil, a product found in most processed foods, my account for as much as 20% of the calorie intake in the average American diet! Checking labels and limiting these items will also help lower the intake of omega-6. Simply by reducing the consumption of omega-6 fats we boost our body's immunities by increasing the production of anti-inflammatory cells. Once again...check those labels!

In order to increase your energy, concentrate on eating foods that are low in the omega-6 fats. Healthy vegetables and fruits, in addition to gluten-free products, may potentially increase your stamina while warding off inflammation that may lead to allergic reactions, illness, and disease.

Lists of Foods that Help Decrease Inflammation

My overall objective is helping you live a healthy life. We've discussed the potential consequences of inflammation and have learned a little about beneficial proteins and fats. The following is a list of several 'super foods' specifically designed to fight inflammation.

Lists of Ten Foods that Help Decrease Inflammation (Listed in Alphabetical Order)
Almonds - A high fiber food, almonds provide protein, fiber, healthy fats, as well as anti-oxidants. (One to two handfuls of salt and gluten free sugar free almonds a day provide several nutritional benefits).
Beans - Red beans, black beans, and kidney beans have earned the reputation for being some of the top-ten richest anti-oxidants around! In addition, certain beans are known to be rich in a compound (beta-glucans) that help reduce the impact on blood sugar levels by slowing down the digestion of carbohydrates. (Gradually increase the amounts if you've been eating a diet low in fiber)
Blueberries - Blueberries are also an excellent source of antioxidants, shown to reduce inflammation in several recent studies.
Green Tea - Green tea is loaded with anti-oxidants. Countless studies have demonstrated that people who regularly drink green tea have significantly less inflammation that those who don't! (Three cups of strong green tea may provide you with an excellent anti-oxidant.)

Ginger - Ginger has been shown to be an effective way to reduce inflammation, as well as an effective treatment for high levels of blood sugar
Olive Oil - Another great anti-inflammatory, one of the mono-unsaturated fats with beneficial properties, known to help fight inflammation!
Papaya - Papaya contains an enzyme called 'papain' that has the ability to break proteins down better than any other food around. Pharmaceutical companies are including papain in more Western medicines to help reduce inflammation. Please be aware that papaya is high in sugar. Ideally it can be eaten a few times a week in order to help stabilize blood sugar and reduce inflammation.
Red Wine - Red wine contains one of the most effective anti-inflammatory chemicals around. Red wine combined with olive oil provides an effective anti-inflammatory team. The red wine stops inflammation in its tracks while olive oil closes the deal, in the event that any inflammation manages to break through! (One small glass per day is recommended for individuals who are able to tolerate limited doses of alcohol.)
Vegetables Containing - Antioxidants (Antioxidants are substances found in plant-foods that help to protect cells and tissue from damage and inflammation!) Broccoli, Eggplant, Okra, Spinach, and Tomatoes are good choices. Additionally, almost all vegetables that are dark in color are healthy foods. Some nutritionists recommend at least eight servings each day (with at least one vegetable from this list).
Yogurt - In addition to being a good source for protein, yogurt also helps to control appetites and burn fat. As sugar is often added, make sure to read the label carefully and add berries, another great source for anti-oxidants! (Try two cups of fat-free, sugar free Greek yogurt, daily!)

Chapter Seven: Enhancing the Quality of Mealtimes

Anti-Inflammatory Cooking: A Gluten Free (or Low Gluten Diet)
This is the heart of the matter! We live in a world that is crazy for wheat. Anyone who suffers from mild glucose intolerance to celiac disease can attest to this fact. The average American may have toast, cereal, French toast, or pancakes for breakfast, pasta, pizza, or a sandwich for lunch, and/or for dinner. Many families eat some form of wheat three times a day. The typical family may consume wheat at every meal and then again for snacks and deserts. Most of the wheat that we consume today has been highly processes and refined. Wheat that has been genetically modified may contain a gluten content of approximately 90%. It's also highly probable that much of this overly processed wheat isn't even recognized by our body as a proper nutrient, thus potentially causing inflammation. This reaction may take the form of an allergic reaction, produce arthritic symptoms, and promote disease and general ill health.

In addition, citrus fruits may cause some bodily inflammations in the body; although it's important to remember that everyone responds in different ways. Becoming aware of your body's response to different foods, including gluten, helps to understand how much is safe for your needs and your family's health.

Remember that once you're aware of the foods that are most beneficial for your health, it's still necessary to avoid excessive amounts of overly processed foods, fried foods, and foods that contain hydrogenated oil. Foods that are highly processed often contain additives and preservatives that overtax the body due to their level of toxicity and their loss of nutritional value, because of extended shelf-life!

The Anti-Inflammation Diet in Summary (Gluten Free Version)
While there are no prescribed quantities of foods requirements, learn to pay attention to your body's signals. Stop eating when you feel comfortably satisfied, even if there is still food on your plate. Never skip meals when you are hungry. Strive to include foods that are recommended below with corresponding serving amounts. And follow a meal plan that is based on approximately 40% carbohydrates, 30% healthy fats, and 30% protein.

Eat organically-grown produce whenever possible.

Plan your menu and meals ahead of time and try not to eat any one type of food obsessively.

Check for gluten in all products, if you have decided to reinforce an anti-inflammatory diet with gluten free options.

Vegetables: Vegetables - lightly steamed. Reduce your consumption of uncooked vegetables, salads excluded. Eat a minimum of 1 to 2 helpings of green leafy vegetables every day, though even more is preferred.

The following vegetables are grouped according to their carbohydrate content with group 1 containing the least and group 4 the most carbs. It's preferable to select most of your vegetables from Group 1 and Group 2.

Group 1	Group 2	Group 3	Group 4	To Avoid
Beet Greens Asparagus Broccoli Bean Sprouts Cabbage - Green and Red Cauliflower Celery Lettuce - Green Cucumber Red and Mixed Romaine Radishes Mustard Greens Endive Dandelion Greens and Spinach Swiss Chard Watercress	Beets Turnips Bok Choy Rutabagas Brussels Sprouts Pumpkin Red Pepper Chives Parsley Eggplant Collard Greens Onion Kale Leeks Kohlrabi String Beans Zucchini	Artichokes Winter Squash Green Peas Carrots Parsnips	Sweet Potatoes Yams	Tomatoes Potatoes

Fruits: An anti-inflammatory diet should include 1 to 2 servings of fruit per day. As with the vegetables, plan to primarily include the lower carbohydrate fruits from Group 1 and Group 2.

Group 1	Group 2	Group 3	Group 4	To Avoid
Cantaloupe Melons Strawberries	Apricots, Blackberries, Cranberries, Kiwis Papayas,	Apples Blueberries Cherries Grapes Pears	Bananas Figs Prunes	Citrus Fruits (Lemon is permissible) (Dried fruits should be limited and avoided

Rhubarb	Peaches, Plums, Raspberries	Pineapples, Pomegranates		completely if you are diabetic.)

In addition to corn and rice, gluten-free grains include amaranth, millet, quinoa, sorghum, and teff.

Food Category	Foods to Eat	Foods to Avoid
Grains: Eat one to two cups of cooked gluten-free grains daily if you want to maintain your weight. Gluten-free grains are included in the following group: teff, amaranth, sorghum, millet, quinoa, as well as corn and rice.	Grains (Gluten-Free) Amaranth Barley Brown, Basmati (Rice Flour) Buckwheat (Corn Flour) Millet Oatmeal Quinoa Spelt Sorghum Teff	Avoid products made with wheat including breads, cereals, whole-wheat flour, white flour, and pasta. "Gluten-Free" - avoid barley, rye, and wheat!
Legumes: Submerse legumes in water overnight and simmer slowly the following day.	Adzuki Beans Beans (Pinto, Black and Garbanzo Beans) Lentils, Kidney Fermented Soybeans Mung Beans Split Peas	Monitor tofu intake as it may cause an allergic reaction.
Seafood: Select wild rather than farmed fish. Try to eat three to four servings per week, baked, broiled, or poached. Deep sea and cold water choices provide an excellent source for fatty acids. Fish provide essential omega-3	Cod Sardines Haddock Mackerel Halibut Trout Tuna Summer Flounder	All Shellfish (clams, crab, lobster, and shrimp)

fats.	Wild Salmon	
Meat: Protein included with all meals will help regulate blood sugar levels and maintain energy.	Organic Turkey and Chicken Free-range/organic Buffalo, Lamb, and Meat (Organic) Wild Game, Venison, and Elk	Pork All Beef that isn't organically raised. Limited amounts of free-range beef.
Herbs and Spices	Any herbs and Spices are permissible.	
Sweeteners: Very limited amounts.	Brown Rice Syrup Agave Syrup Stevia Pure Maple Syrup Raw Honey	Absolutely no Nutra-Sweet or any other sweetener is allowed. This includes all sugar.
Butter and Oil: One pound of organic butter can be mixed with a cup of 0.2% olive oil, and then stored as a buttery spread in the refrigerator.	Coconut oil for baking For cooking use olive oil. Organic Butter, in small amounts as a spread. For salads use seed or nut oils.	Hydrogenated oils Partially-hydrogenated oils (trans-fats) Note: Overheating oils may convert oils to Trans-fats.
Beverages	At least one-half of your body weight of filtered water (in fluid oz.) per day. Minimum amounts of soy, almond, oat, and/or rice milk, and herbal teas.	Alcohol Coffee Caffeinated Teas Juice Soda
Dairy Products and Eggs	Eggs - Organic	Commercial eggs Dairy products (Yogurt, cheese, and cow milk in moderation)
Misc.		Products made from corn Fried foods Processed foods

Fast and Easy Gluten Free Recipes

We live in a fast-paced, eat-on-the-go world where our daily work and school schedules often do not provide adequate time to shop, prepare food, and eat in a relaxed way. Our schedules often don't allow for regular meals and healthy snacks. It is not unusual to eat at all hours during the day and often before retiring to bed for the evening. While we sleep, our digestive system isn't functioning at its optimal level, yet we often tax it with one of the largest meals of the day. Our habits also include highly processed, pre-packaged meals, possibly as much as 40% of our diet!

A Four Week Meal Plan

Additionally, for people who experience gluten sensitivity symptoms and gluten allergies, finding the right foods can pose additional problems. Since, as we've learned, most processed foods contain gluten, we often have to search for those foods that are gluten free. We often find ourselves asking "Is this Gluten free?" Therefore, I have included gluten free foods as part of the gluten free diet plan. Hopefully these simple meal ideas and gluten free diet suggestions will help make your meal planning more relaxed and your meals more enjoyable!

Organizing our Gluten Free Life and Cutting our Food Bill

With a gluten free diet, my wife and I came up with a way to simplify our lives while cutting our food bill. As a working couple, we recognize the value of our time and the ever increasing cost of groceries for our families.

One evening, shortly after we switched to a gluten free diet we were discussing the number of hours that we were spending creating a gluten free menu, shopping, and cooking for our family, only to start the whole process again.

Discovering a Better Way

While we were talking, my wife started making a list of menus and recipes. She has always found creative solutions to daily demands by making to-do lists and following through on tasks, especially at work as an activity director. We realized that her list could serve as an enjoyable and helpful tool for feeding our growing family a gluten free diet while saving money! We also found that having a plan not only helps to save money; it eliminates the late afternoon frustration of from having to decide what to serve for dinner.

Our Strategy

As we talked, we found that for the majority of meals we were recycling the same recipes. So we started by making a list of thirty gluten-free family favorites. For the most part, we included foods that our families preferred, easy and quick to prepare recipes.

We found that the recipes fell into a few categories: vegetarian, meat/chicken, salads/supper sandwiches, easy skillet and crock-pot meals, and pasta dishes. We listed main entrees in these categories until we reached 30 meals that each of our families especially enjoyed. Another key consideration was expense. Selecting less expensive ingredients substantially cut our food bill!

Filling in the Blanks

Next we prepared a monthly calendar. (I have included a sample at the end of this section.) At the top of each calendar square, we wrote down the meal that we had designated for that day. We factored in game/practice days, evening meetings, and dates when we were expecting guests. Our goal was to include as many daily gluten-free meal requirements as possible. Below each main-meal entry, we included side-dishes that would add to our gluten free meals.

The final step was to create a gluten-free grocery list that could be used and reused. The beauty of this was that each time we shopped we could print out a new list and simply check off what we needed to complete our meal requirements each month. Remember to include foods for breakfast, snacks, and lunch. You'll probably find there's a definite pattern to these meals. To create your four week meal plan, simply follow these recommendations for the next two months and keep track of the changes!

Final Thoughts

It may help to have two different gluten free meal plans, one for winter and summer meals. It's also possible to remain flexible. If something unexpected comes up, simply swap out the meals. Photocopying pages from cookbooks may be helpful. My wife came up with the idea of creating her own cookbook from a three-ring binder with plastic page sleeves and marked sections.

...

Chapter Eight: Foods and Substitution

Sample Gluten Free List – Shopping

Gluten Free Baking/Cereals	Gluten Free Breads	Fruits and Vegetables
gluten free grains	gluten free buns	bean sprouts, broccoli
gluten free rice	gluten free biscuits	red pepper
gluten free oatmeal	gluten free Rolls	cabbage: red and green
gluten free oats	gluten free muffins	leeks /onion
gluten free spaghetti	gluten free wheat bread	asparagus
gluten free macaroni		rutabagas, turnips
gluten free Cornbread		string beans
gluten free noodles		zucchini
gluten free Stuffing		lettuce - green, mixed,
gluten free Cereals		cantaloupe
gluten free Granola		melons
gluten free pasta		strawberries
gluten free flour		rhubarb

Gluten Free Dairy - Eggs	Gluten free Snacks/Desserts	Gluten Free Drinks/ Misc.
gluten free cheese	gluten free Crackers	gluten free drinks
gluten free ice cream	gluten free cupcakes	gluten free beer
gluten free milk	gluten free brownies	gluten free alcohol

organic eggs	gluten free cakes	
gluten free butter spreads	gluten free cookies	
	gluten free chocolate	
Meats/Poultry	**Soups/Sauces/Spreads/Condiments**	**Frozen Foods**
gluten free chicken	gluten free soups	gluten free pancakes
organic meats	gluten free sauces	gluten free Pastry
	gluten free peanut butter	
	olive oil	

(Chart - what to eliminate, what to substitute, and the directions)

Foods To Eliminate	Food Substitutions	How to Substitute
Butter	Blend organic butter and virgin olive oil (as a spread). Blend organic butter and coconut oil (for baking). Non-hydrogenated vegan margarine	Equal quantities may be substituted.
Eggs - Commercial	Many people tolerate organic eggs the following binders may also be substituted. Soaked Flaxseeds (overnight in water or boiled for 15 min. Tofu - great substitute in scrambles or baked goods Banana binds baked goods (sweet in taste) Arrowroot powder (a binder for gluten-free flours) Guar gum (very small amount) Xanthan gum	1 to 2 tablespoons seeds in ½ to 1 cup water ¼ cup for 1 egg ½ to 1 banana for cookies or muffins 1 tablespoon for each cup of Gluten-free flour ¼ to ½ teaspoon for baked goods

	Xanthan gum	1 teaspoon per cup of gluten free flour
Chocolate	Carob powder – nutritionally better than chocolate!	3 tablespoons for every ounce of chocolate
Cow's milk	almond milk (or other nut milk), oat milk, rice milk, sesame seed milk, soy milk	Equal quantities may be substituted
Peanuts and peanut butter	Almonds and almond butter	Equal quantities
Potatoes	Jerusalem artichokes, yucca root, taro root	Cook in a similar manner to potatoes.
Sugar	Honey tends to be twice as sweet as processed cane sugar. Pure Maple syrup Brown rice syrup Stevia	½ amount recipe calls for ½ to ¾ amount recipe calls for ½ to ¾ amount recipe calls for Very small amounts conversions on label
Wheat	Note: When any of these flours are substituted, you may need to add slightly more baking soda or baking powder to increase rising. Amaranth (usually has a strong flavor) Barley (small amount of gluten) Garbanzo Kamut (gluten)	Requires a binder May require a binder No binder is necessary No binder required

	Oat (very small amounts of gluten)	May require a binder
	Quinoa (bitter, best when mixed with other flours)	
	Rice (can be grainy; mix with other flours)	Requires a binder
	Rye (contains gluten; should not be eaten every day)	Requires a binder
	Soy (can have a beany flavor)	No binder required
	Spelt (contains gluten; should not be eaten every day)	Requires a binder
		No binder required

Modifying Recipes for an Anti-Inflammatory Gluten-Free Diet

Sample modified cookie recipe:

Following is a general guideline for adapting and modifying recipes to suit both anti-inflammatory and gluten free diet. My wife, and I, found that making these changes took a little practice. Climate and altitude also make some difference, so you will have to experiment with the techniques. Before you know it, though, you'll be cooking like the pros!

Fruit/Nut Cookies:

Original "gluten-heavy" recipe
6 cups white flour
1 1/2 cups brown sugar
1 1/2 cups white sugar
4 eggs
2 cups butter or shortening
1 teaspoon salt
1 teaspoon baking soda
2 bag chocolate chips
You'll need to adapt the sugar and flour requirements in the following way...
3 cups gluten free flour
1 1/2 cups honey
1 cup organic butter
1 teaspoon sea salt
1 teaspoon aluminum-free baking soda
4 organic eggs (or 2 mashed banana with 6 tablespoons ground

Flax-seeds soaked in 1/2 cup water overnight)
2 cup seeds and/or nuts
1 cup cut-up fruit such apples, dates, and apples

Please notice that we've reduced the butter by half and replaced the chocolate chips with seeds, fruit, and nuts. If you prefer a flatter cookie, increase the amount of butter. These cookies are filling and help to stabilize the blood sugar levels. This new cookie contains some. A little added cinnamon helps in maintaining a balanced glucose level. There are many great possibilities for added ingredients!

Lists of Items to be kept on Hand Always

The following is a list of ingredients that are helpful to keep on hand. You can add to your list over time, to avoid buying everything at once.

1. Almond butter
2. Beans and legumes, canned or dried
3. Brown rice, quinoa, oats, amaranth, other grains
4. Brown rice syrup
5. Coconut oil (organic) for baking
6. Dried herbs and spices
7. Extra-virgin, cold-pressed olive oil
8. Filtered water
9. Fresh vegetables
10. Fresh fruits
11. Garlic
12. Gluten free flours
13. Lemons
14. Milk substitutes such as rice milk, oat milk, soy milk, almond milk
15. Nuts and seeds
16. Onions
17. Rice, organic apple, balsamic, tarragon vinegars
18. Pure maple syrup
19. Raw honey and/or agave syrup
20. Large skillet or wok to stir-fry vegetables
21. Large pot for sauces and soups
22. Two-quart saucepan for cooking rice and other grains
23. A good appetite and JOY!

Chapter Nine: Simplified and Effective Dietary Plan

Patients/Members of the family who are suffering from heart disease, arthritis, dementia, and allergies...
are included in this program! The beauty is that even though the anti-inflammation gluten free-diet is designed to include specific foods, the program can easily be adapted to meet specific individual needs. I have included a food journal so that you can keep track of your personal dietary needs and track progress, make adjustments, and learn more efficiently identify your unique dietary needs as well as those of family members. You will want to include the specialized recommendations of your family doctor.

Food Journal:

Monday:
Tuesday:
Wednesday:
Thursday:
Friday:
Saturday:
Sunday:
Notes:

Chapter Ten: Anti-inflammation Recipes & Meal Planning

When it comes to eating right and exercising, there is no "I'll start tomorrow." Tomorrow is disease.

Terri Guillemets

The following chart shows a sample anti-inflammatory menu for one week. The program that my wife and I designed allows for meal flexibility. The anti-inflammation gluten-free diet is less of a diet than a healthy eating program. The beauty is that it can be adapted to suit the needs and dietary requirements of your family. I have deliberately not included specific food allotments for that reason. The purpose of this book is to help increase your awareness of the impact that diet has on our lives. Whether you are searching for an anti-inflammatory diet, a gluten-free diet, or a combination of both, this book is designed just for you. The heart of the matter is to live a well-balanced life! Move more, drink the right amount of fresh, filtered water and eat a healthy balance of fruits, vegetables, organic/home grown eggs and poultry/meat, fresh cold water and farmed fish, the dairy or soy products, and grains that are right for you. After four weeks of following this guide, your body will let you know!

Sample Anti-Inflammatory Menus for a Week

	Monday	Tuesday	Wed.	Thursday	Friday
Breakfast	10-minute Blueberry Oatmeal	Breakfast Egg Scramble	Blueberry Buckwheat Pancakes	Gluten Free Banana Bread	Gluten Free Almond Raspberry Danish Tartle
Morning Snack	Carob Chip Cookies	Gluten-Free Almond Butter and Banana Sandwiches	Citrus Berry Parfait	Gluten-Free Chocolate Cupcakes	Garbanzo Bean Chocol Cake
Lunch	Gluten-Free Cream of Mushroom	Hot Summer Chili	Salmon Egg Salad	Fruity Chicken Salad	Cedar Planked Salm Fillets

	Soup					
Snack	Berry Medley Walnut Parfait with Coconut Vanilla Ice Cream	GF crackers Peanut butter	Gluten free nut/seed cookies	GF Fruit ice cream	Protein drink	
Dinner	Gluten-Free Teriyaki Salmon	Honey Mustard Grilled Pork Chops	Beef Stuffed Cabbage	Raw Veggie Nuts and Seeds Salad	Parmigi Beef Meatb	

Anti-Inflammatory/Gluten Free (Dinner) Menus for Four Weeks

Week	Monday	Tuesday	Wednesday	Thursday	Friday	
Week 1	Spinach N' Mushroom Stuffed Chicken	Gluten-Free Teriyaki Salmon	Grilled Tilapia with Black Bean Mango Salsa	Honey Mustard Grilled Pork Chops	Grilled Lemon N' Lime Cod Fillets	Stuf
Week 2	Raw Veggie Nuts and Seeds Salad	Lemon and Herb Crusted Salmon Fillets	Parmigiano Beef Meatballs	Spicy Almond Fish Sticks with Garlic Lime Tartar Sauce	Grilled Rosemary Lime Swordfish	Mus Mar Chic
Week 3	Roasted Pork Tenderloin with Blueberry	Gluten-Free Beef and Broccoli Stir-fry	Spinach N' Mushroom Stuffed Chicken	Beef Stuffed Cabbage	Gluten-Free Teriyaki Salmon	Lem Cod

		Sauce					
Week 4	Grilled Tilapia with Black Bean Mango Salsa	Raw Veggie Nuts and Seeds Salad	Gluten-Free Grilled Pineapple Burgers	Lemon and Herb Crusted Salmon Fillets	Honey-Mustard Lemon Marinated Chicken	Bee	

Conclusion "A Healthy Future"
Dear Reader,

In conclusion, your body will always let you know what is best! If you're experiencing pain and sleepless nights (as I was), or breaking out in hives (as our daughter did, it's time to make a change! The Anti-Inflammatory Gluten-Free Path to Better Health will guide you along the right track.

I cannot guarantee that you will live a disease free, allergy, inflammatory free life, but I do believe that applying the principles in this book will improve your overall health and help ward off future ailments. If nothing else, I believe that you will begin to feel and look better and

53 Delicious Anti-Inflammation Recipes to Keep Your Family Healthy

BREAKFAST

1. 10-minute Blueberry Oatmeal
Servings: 2
Serving size: 1 medium bowl
Preparation time: 5 minutes
Cook time: 5 minutes
Ready in: 10 minutes

Nutrition Facts

Serving Size 264 g

Amount Per Serving

Calories 392   Calories from Fat 63

                                                       % Daily Value*

Total Fat 7.0g	**11%**
Saturated Fat 2.2g	**11%**
Trans Fat 0.0g	
Cholesterol 10mg	**3%**
Sodium 52mg	**2%**
Total Carbohydrates 76.7g	**26%**
Dietary Fiber 6.1g	**24%**
Sugars 47.6g	
Protein 10.2g	

Vitamin A 1%   •   Vitamin C 10%
Calcium 3%   •   Iron 13%

Nutrition Grade C+

* Based on a 2000 calorie diet

Ingredients

- 1 cup 2% or skim milk
- 1 cup gluten-free quick-cooking oats
- 1/4 cup raw honey
- 1/2 teaspoon ground cinnamon
- ½ teaspoon pure vanilla extract
- 3/4 cup fresh or frozen unsweetened blueberries, thawed
- 1 tablespoon sliced almonds

Directions

1. **Place** a saucepan in medium heat. Add milk and bring to a boil.
2. **Stir** in the oats and cook for 2 minutes, or until thick, stirring occasionally. Add the honey, cinnamon, and vanilla and blend well.
3. **Ladle** oatmeal into bowls and top with blueberries.

2. Breakfast Egg Scramble
Servings: 4
Preparation time: 5 minutes
Cook time: 8 minutes
Ready in: 13 minutes

Nutrition Facts

Serving Size 130 g

Amount Per Serving

Calories 103	Calories from Fat 55

	% Daily Value*
Total Fat 6.1g	**9%**
Saturated Fat 2.0g	**10%**
Cholesterol 7mg	**2%**
Sodium 105mg	**4%**
Total Carbohydrates 6.4g	**2%**
Dietary Fiber 1.7g	**7%**
Sugars 3.2g	
Protein 6.5g	

Vitamin A 22%	Vitamin C 91%
Calcium 6%	Iron 3%

Nutrition Grade B+

* Based on a 2000 calorie diet

Ingredients

- 4 organic free-range eggs, beaten
- 1 tomato, seeded and chopped
- 1 pinch salt and pepper, or to taste
- 1/4 cup gluten-free Cheddar cheese, grated
- 1/2 cup broccoli florets, chopped
- 1 medium red bell pepper, diced
- 1 medium onion, chopped
- 2 cloves garlic, crushed and chopped

- 1 tablespoon olive oil

Directions

1. **Heat** olive oil in a skillet over medium-high heat. Add garlic and onion and sauté until garlic is lightly browned and onion is soft.
2. **Stir** in broccoli and cook for about 5 minutes, or until tender. Turn heat to medium. Add the beaten eggs and cook for 2 minutes.
3. **Mix** in the tomato and red bell pepper. Season with salt and pepper. Stir occasionally and cook until eggs are set. Serve warm with sprinkled cheese on top.

3. Blueberry Buckwheat Pancakes
Servings: 8
Serving size: 1 pancake
Preparation time: 5 minutes
Cook time: 15 minutes
Ready in: 20 minutes

Nutrition Facts

Serving Size 66 g

Amount Per Serving

Calories 282	Calories from Fat 150

	% Daily Value*
Total Fat 16.7g	**26%**
Saturated Fat 14.6g	**73%**
Trans Fat 0.0g	
Cholesterol 0mg	**0%**
Sodium 197mg	**8%**
Total Carbohydrates 32.2g	**11%**
Dietary Fiber 6.8g	**27%**
Sugars 11.9g	
Protein 4.3g	

Vitamin A 0%	•	Vitamin C 2%
Calcium 2%	•	Iron 10%

Nutrition Grade C+

*Based on a 2000 calorie diet

Ingredients
- 1 teaspoon coconut oil
- 1 3/4 cup organic coconut butter (recommended: Artisana)
- 1 1/2 cup buckwheat flour
- 1/8 teaspoon salt
- 3 tablespoon raw honey
- 1 teaspoon baking soda
- 2 tablespoon pure maple syrup

- 1/4 cup frozen blueberries

Directions

1. **Combine** the buckwheat flour, salt, honey, and baking soda in a large mixing bowl.
2. **Whisk** together the egg and 1 1/2 cup coconut butter. Add egg mixture to the buckwheat batter gently. Let the batter stand for 10 minutes (or overnight).
3. **Place** a saucepan over medium heat. Add 1 teaspoon of coconut butter and melt.
4. **Ladle** 1/4 cup of batter onto the pan to for each pancake. Turn the pancakes over once bubbles burst on top; cook the other side until golden brown. Place pancakes in serving plates and top with 1 teaspoon each of the remaining butter and frozen blueberries.

4. Gluten Free Banana Bread
Servings: 8
Preparation time: 10 minutes
Cook time: 20-30 minutes
Ready in: 30 minutes

Nutrition Facts

Serving Size 176 g

Amount Per Serving

Calories 392	Calories from Fat 163
	% Daily Value*
Total Fat 18.1g	**28%**
Saturated Fat 12.4g	**62%**
Trans Fat 0.0g	
Cholesterol 41mg	**14%**
Sodium 137mg	**6%**
Total Carbohydrates 56.5g	**19%**
Dietary Fiber 4.4g	**18%**
Sugars 24.3g	
Protein 5.8g	
Vitamin A 2%	Vitamin C 13%
Calcium 7%	Iron 11%

Nutrition Grade B-

* Based on a 2000 calorie diet

Ingredients

- 1 cup white rice
- 1/2 cup ground oats
- 1/4 cup almond meal
- 1/4 cup flax meal
- 1 teaspoon baking powder
- 1/2 teaspoon sea salt
- 1/2 cup coconut oil, melted, and 1 tablespoon for greasing

- 1/4 cup raw honey
- 6 ripe bananas, mashed
- 2 organic free-range eggs, lightly beaten
- 3 tablespoons maple syrup
- 1 teaspoon cinnamon
- 1 pinch nutmeg

Directions

1. **Preheat** oven to 350 degrees F. Grease a 9x5 inch loaf pan lightly with 1 tablespoon coconut oil.
2. **Mix** together the white rice, ground oats, almond meal, flax meal, baking powder and salt in a large mixing bowl. In another large bowl, stir together the eggs, coconut oil, honey, maple syrup, cinnamon, nutmeg, and bananas. Add the flour mixture and mix well to produce a moist batter. Transfer batter to the loaf pan.
3. **Bake** for 20-30 minutes, or until a toothpick inserted into center of the loaf comes out clean or with only a few crumbs sticking to it. If using muffin or cupcake tins, bake for 15 minutes, or until a toothpick inserted into the center of a muffin comes out clean.

5. Gluten Free Almond-Raspberry Danish Tartlets

Servings: 12
Serving size: 1 tartlet
Preparation time: 20 minutes
Cook time: 10-12 minutes
Ready in: 30 minutes

Nutrition Facts

Serving Size 38 g

Amount Per Serving

Calories 129	Calories from Fat 74

% Daily Value*

Total Fat 8.2g	**13%**
Saturated Fat 3.3g	**16%**
Trans Fat 0.0g	
Cholesterol 0mg	**0%**
Sodium 94mg	**4%**
Total Carbohydrates 12.8g	**4%**
Dietary Fiber 1.3g	**5%**
Sugars 4.3g	
Protein 2.7g	

Vitamin A 0%	▪	Vitamin C 1%
Calcium 3%	▪	Iron 4%

Nutrition Grade D+

* Based on a 2000 calorie diet

Ingredients
Crust and Filling:

- 2 cups gluten-free pancake mix
- 1/4 cup almond butter, room temperature
- 2 tablespoons Stevia
- 2/3 cup almond milk
- 1/2 teaspoon almond extract
- 1/4 cup organic raspberry jam

Glaze and Garnish:
- 2/3 cup Stevia
- 2 tablespoons milk, or more as needed
- 1/2 teaspoon pure vanilla extract
- 1/4 teaspoon almond extract
- 1/2 cup chopped almonds

Directions

1. **Preheat** an oven to 400 degrees F (200 degrees C). Line a baking sheet with parchment paper.
2. **Make the crusts**: In a large mixing bowl, mix together the pancake mix, butter, and 2 tablespoons Stevia until crumbly. Stir in 2/3 cup milk and 1/2 teaspoon almond extract; mix well to incorporate. Drop several tablespoonful of dough onto the baking sheet; place each dough ball 2 inches apart. Make a hollow on each dough ball by pressing the back of a teaspoon in the center.
3. **Fill** each center with 1 teaspoon of raspberry jam. Bake for 10-12 minutes, or until lightly browned.
4. **Make the glaze**: Stir together all the glaze ingredients (except for the chopped almonds) until smooth. Drizzle the glaze over the tartlets and sprinkle chopped almonds over the top.

6. Breakfast Gluten-free Brownies
Servings: 12
Serving size: 1 brownie
Preparation time: 15 minutes
Cook time: 20 minutes
Ready in: 35 minutes

Nutrition Facts

Serving Size 105 g

Amount Per Serving

Calories 267	Calories from Fat 88

	% Daily Value*
Total Fat 9.8g	**15%**
Saturated Fat 5.6g	**28%**
Trans Fat 0.0g	
Cholesterol 18mg	**6%**
Sodium 78mg	**3%**
Total Carbohydrates 39.0g	**13%**
Dietary Fiber 6.1g	**24%**
Sugars 23.9g	
Protein 6.3g	
Vitamin A 1%	Vitamin C 2%
Calcium 9%	Iron 6%

Nutrition Grade D+

* Based on a 2000 calorie diet

Ingredients

- 1 1/2 cups gluten-free quick-cooking oats
- 3/4 cup carob powder
- 1/2 cup gluten-free all-purpose baking flour
- 1 teaspoon baking powder
- 3/4 cup raw honey
- 3/4 cup flax seed meal
- 1/2 teaspoon ground cinnamon

- 1/4 teaspoon salt
- 1/4 cup rice milk
- 1 teaspoon pure vanilla extract
- 1 organic free-range egg
- 1 ripe banana, mashed
- 1 tablespoon coconut oil for greasing

Directions

1. **Preheat** oven to 350 degrees F (175 degrees C). Lightly grease an 8x10-inch baking pan.
2. **In a large mixing bowl, combine** the first 8 ingredients. In another mixing bowl, stir together the rice milk, vanilla, and banana. Stir in the banana mixture into flour mixture. Transfer batter into the prepared baking pan.
3. **Bake** for about 20 minutes, or until a toothpick inserted in the center comes out clean. Cover pan and allow brownies to cool for at least 5 minutes. Slice into bars and serve.

7. Spinach and Berries Smoothie

Servings: 4
Preparation time: 5 minutes
Cook time: 5 minutes
Ready in: 10 minutes

Nutrition Facts

Serving Size 152 g

Amount Per Serving

Calories 99	Calories from Fat 14

	% Daily Value*
Total Fat 1.5g	**2%**
Trans Fat 0.0g	
Cholesterol 1mg	**0%**
Sodium 52mg	**2%**
Total Carbohydrates 17.6g	**6%**
Dietary Fiber 3.0g	**12%**
Sugars 12.2g	
Protein 4.4g	
Vitamin A 15% •	Vitamin C 23%
Calcium 10% •	Iron 4%

Nutrition Grade A

* Based on a 2000 calorie diet

Ingredients

- 1/2 cup frozen strawberries
- 1/2 cup frozen blueberries
- 1 cup fresh spinach leaves, chopped
- 1 ripe banana, peeled and chopped
- 1/2 cup soy milk
- 1/2 cup fat-free plain yogurt
- 1 1/2 tablespoons flax seeds
- 1 teaspoon honey

Directions
Combine all ingredients in a blender and blend until smooth. Pour into glasses and serve.

8. Quick Scrambled Egg N' Mushrooms

Servings: 6
Preparation time: 5 minutes
Cook time: 5 minutes
Ready in: 10 minutes

Nutrition Facts

Serving Size 72 g

Amount Per Serving

Calories 142	Calories from Fat 115

	% Daily Value*
Total Fat 12.8g	20%
Saturated Fat 2.6g	13%
Cholesterol 164mg	55%
Sodium 62mg	3%
Total Carbohydrates 1.8g	1%
Sugars 0.9g	
Protein 5.9g	

Vitamin A 7%	•	Vitamin C 12%
Calcium 3%	•	Iron 6%

Nutrition Grade B-
* Based on a 2000 calorie diet

Ingredients

- 1/4 cup olive oil
- 3 cloves garlic, crushed and chopped
- 1/4 cup onions, chopped
- 1/4 cup green bell peppers, chopped
- 1/4 cup fresh mushrooms, sliced
- 6 eggs, beaten
- 1/4 cup fresh tomato, chopped
- salt and freshly ground black pepper, to taste

Directions

1. **Place** a skillet over medium-high heat. Add the olive oil. Once oil is hot, add the garlic and sauté until lightly browned.
2. **Stir** in the mushrooms, onions, bell peppers, and tomatoes and cook until onions are soft. Stir in the beaten eggs and cook for 1 minute, or until egg is set.
3. **Slice** into wedges and serve.

9. Gluten-free Sugar-free Granola

Servings: 10
Serving size: 1 cup
Preparation time: 10 minutes
Cook time: 12 minutes
Ready in: 22 minutes

Nutrition Facts

Serving Size 155 g

Amount Per Serving

Calories 658　　　　Calories from Fat 312

	% Daily Value*
Total Fat 34.7g	**53%**
Saturated Fat 5.2g	**26%**
Trans Fat 0.0g	
Cholesterol 0mg	**0%**
Sodium 206mg	**9%**
Total Carbohydrates 75.9g	**25%**
Dietary Fiber 12.8g	**51%**
Sugars 11.9g	
Protein 16.6g	
Vitamin A 1% •	Vitamin C 3%
Calcium 23% •	Iron 37%

Nutrition Grade D+

* Based on a 2000 calorie diet

Ingredients

- 5 cups gluten-free rolled oats
- 2 cups unsalted almonds, chopped
- 1 cup unsalted hazelnuts, chopped
- 3/4 cup sesame seeds
- 2 teaspoons ground cinnamon
- 1 teaspoon ground nutmeg
- 1 teaspoon sea salt

- 1/2 cup dried dates
- 1/2 cup dried prunes
- 1/2 cup dried cranberries
- 3/4 cup agave syrup (or raw honey)
- 1 tablespoon pure vanilla extract
- 2 tablespoons coconut oil

Directions

1. **Preheat** the oven to 350°.
2. **In a large roasting pan, combine** the oats, almonds, hazelnuts, and sesame seeds, and then stir in the cinnamon, nutmeg, and salt. Add the dried fruits and toss well. Drizzle mixture with maple syrup, vanilla, and coconut oil, and toss to coat.
3. **Bake** for 12 minutes. Stir with a fork once halfway through. Let cool and serve.

10. No-Bake Carob Mousse Cake

Servings: 5
Preparation time: 15 minutes

Nutrition Facts

Serving Size 120 g

Amount Per Serving

Calories 340	Calories from Fat 125

	% Daily Value*
Total Fat 13.9g	**21%**
Saturated Fat 7.0g	**35%**
Trans Fat 0.0g	
Cholesterol 0mg	**0%**
Sodium 63mg	**3%**
Total Carbohydrates 53.6g	**18%**
Dietary Fiber 6.2g	**25%**
Sugars 33.1g	
Protein 4.8g	

Vitamin A 1%	Vitamin C 8%
Calcium 9%	Iron 6%

Nutrition Grade C-

* Based on a 2000 calorie diet

Ingredients
Crust:

- 1/4 cup raw walnuts, chopped
- 1 cup dates, pitted
- 1/4 cup carob powder
- 1/2 teaspoon pure vanilla extract
- 2 teaspoon water
- 1 pinch salt

Mousse:

- 3/4 cup avocado, chopped
- 1/4 cup carob powder
- 1 ripe banana
- 2 tablespoons agave syrup
- 1/2 teaspoon pure vanilla extract

Directions

1. **Place** all ingredients for the crust in a blender or food processor and process until a dough consistency is reached. Using your hands, press down the dough in a shallow dish.
2. **Process** all mousse ingredients in a blender or food processor until creamy.
3. **Pour** mousse over the crust. Place cake in the refrigerator to chill.

11. Summer Fresh Fruit Salad
Servings: 5-6
Serving size: 1 medium bowl
Preparation time: 15 minutes
Ready in: 15 minutes

Nutrition Facts

Serving Size 394 g

Amount Per Serving

Calories 290   Calories from Fat 10

	% Daily Value*
Total Fat 1.1g	**2%**
Cholesterol 0mg	**0%**
Sodium 24mg	**1%**
Total Carbohydrates 72.6g	**24%**
Dietary Fiber 8.0g	**32%**
Sugars 49.1g	
Protein 3.8g	

Vitamin A 54%   •   Vitamin C 155%
Calcium 6%   •   Iron 12%

Nutrition Grade A

* Based on a 2000 calorie diet

Ingredients

- 6 bananas, peeled and sliced
- 2 cups strawberries, hulled and halved
- 2 cups cantaloupe balls
- 1/2 cup seedless green grapes
- 2 ripe bananas, sliced
- 1/2 cup blackberries or blueberries

Dressing:

- 1/2 cup nonfat lemon yogurt

- 1/4 cup raw honey
- 1/2 cup fresh lemon juice
- 5 sprigs fresh mint, chopped

Directions

1. **Place** fruits in a large bowl.
2. **Combine** dressing ingredients in a small bowl and pour over fruits. Gently toss to coat.
3. **Cover** and refrigerate before serving.

12. Avocado Omelet

Servings: 4
Preparation time: 8 minutes
Cook time: 15 minutes
Ready in: 23 minutes

Nutrition Facts

Serving Size 252 g

Amount Per Serving

Calories 295   Calories from Fat 210

% Daily Value*

Total Fat 23.3g	**36%**
Saturated Fat 4.8g	**24%**
Cholesterol 327mg	**109%**
Sodium 147mg	**6%**
Total Carbohydrates 10.8g	**4%**
Dietary Fiber 5.1g	**20%**
Sugars 3.6g	
Protein 13.8g	

Vitamin A 52% • Vitamin C 41%
Calcium 8% • Iron 20%

Nutrition Grade A-

* Based on a 2000 calorie diet

Ingredients

- 2 cloves garlic, crushed and chopped
- 1/2 cup mushroom, diced
- 1 large tomato, diced
- 1 medium onion, chopped
- 3 cups baby spinach leaves, chopped
- 1 avocado flesh, mashed
- 8 eggs
- salt and pepper to taste

- 2 tablespoons olive oil

Directions

1. **Heat** olive oil in a skillet over medium heat. Add the garlic and sauté until lightly browned.
2. **Stir** in the mushroom, tomato, onion, spinach, and mashed avocado; season with a pinch of salt and pepper.
3. **Cook** vegetables until tender. In a medium bowl, beat the eggs and season with salt and pepper.
4. **Pour** the egg mixture in the skillet and cook for 3 minutes on each side, or until set.

13. Flax-Almond Porridge
Servings: 2-4
Serving size: 1 medium bowl
Preparation time: 5 minutes
Cook time: 4 minutes
Ready in: 9 minutes

Nutrition Facts

Serving Size 271 g

Amount Per Serving

Calories 543	Calories from Fat 361

	% Daily Value*
Total Fat 40.1g	**62%**
Saturated Fat 26.1g	**131%**
Trans Fat 0.0g	
Cholesterol 0mg	**0%**
Sodium 21mg	**1%**
Total Carbohydrates 47.4g	**16%**
Dietary Fiber 9.7g	**39%**
Sugars 29.8g	
Protein 8.7g	

Vitamin A 1%	•	Vitamin C 18%
Calcium 10%	•	Iron 19%

Nutrition Grade B-

* Based on a 2000 calorie diet

Ingredients

- 2 bananas, mashed
- 2 cups almond milk
- 1 teaspoon raw honey
- 3/4 cup almond meal
- 1/4 cup flax meal
- 1 teaspoon ground cinnamon
- 1/4 cup organic pure maple syrup

- 1 apple, diced

Directions

1. **Place** a saucepan over medium heat. Add and stir together almond meal, flax meal, almond milk, honey, and bananas until smooth. Sprinkle cinnamon over mixture.
2. **Simmer** for about 3-4 minutes, or until thick and bubbly.
3. **Pour** porridge into bowls. Add diced apples on top and drizzle with maple syrup.

14. Banana and Blueberry French Toast
Servings: 6-8
Preparation time: 10 minutes
Cook time: 6 minutes
Ready in: 16 minutes

Nutrition Facts

Serving Size 103 g

Amount Per Serving

Calories 193   Calories from Fat 73

	% Daily Value*
Total Fat 8.1g	**12%**
Saturated Fat 5.1g	**26%**
Trans Fat 0.0g	
Cholesterol 143mg	**48%**
Sodium 71mg	**3%**
Total Carbohydrates 26.8g	**9%**
Dietary Fiber 1.3g	**5%**
Sugars 19.2g	
Protein 4.7g	

Vitamin A 4%   •   Vitamin C 4%
Calcium 4%   •   Iron 6%

Nutrition Grade C-

* Based on a 2000 calorie diet

Ingredients

- 1 tablespoon coconut oil (for greasing)
- 1 loaf gluten-free sliced bread
- 4 organic free-range eggs
- 1 teaspoon cinnamon
- 1 dash salt
- 1/4 cup coconut milk or almond milk
- 1/2 cup organic pure maple syrup

- 1/2 cup frozen blueberries
- 1/2 cup sliced ripe bananas

Directions

1. **Preheat** a skillet to 350 degrees F.
2. **Beat** together eggs, cinnamon, sea salt, and coconut milk in a medium bowl. Grease a skillet with coconut oil and place over medium heat.
3. **Coat** each bread slice with the egg mixture and cook each side in the skillet for 3-4 minutes.
4. **Place** toasts in serving plates and top with blueberries and bananas, then drizzle maple syrup over the top.

15. Pan Fried Halibut with Cilantro Tartar Sauce

Servings: 4
Serving size: 1 fish fillet and 1/4 cup cilantro tartar sauce
Preparation time: 45 minutes
Cook time: 10 minutes
Ready in: 55 minutes

Nutrition Facts

Serving Size 278 g

Amount Per Serving

Calories 632	Calories from Fat 250

% Daily Value*

Total Fat 27.8g	**43%**
Saturated Fat 9.4g	**47%**
Trans Fat 0.0g	
Cholesterol 147mg	**49%**
Sodium 763mg	**32%**
Total Carbohydrates 25.7g	**9%**
Dietary Fiber 15.3g	**61%**
Sugars 3.7g	
Protein 54.5g	

Vitamin A 9%	Vitamin C 5%
Calcium 11%	Iron 25%

Nutrition Grade B

* Based on a 2000 calorie diet

Ingredients

Fish fillet:

- 4 halibut fillets, skinless (or any white fish)
- 2 eggs
- 1 1/2 cups coconut flour
- 1 tablespoon garam masala
- 1 teaspoon salt

- 1/2 teaspoon freshly ground black pepper
- 1 teaspoon garlic powder
- 1/4 cup olive oil

Cilantro Tartar Sauce:

- 2 tablespoons fresh cilantro
- 1 cup gluten-free mayonnaise
- 1/4 cup onion, finely chopped
- 1 tablespoon lemon juice
- 1/2 teaspoon dried dill

Directions

1. **Stir** together all tartar sauce ingredients and chill for 30 minutes.
2. **Beat** the eggs in a bowl. In a separate bowl, stir together the coconut flour, garam masala, salt, garlic powder, and pepper. Coat each side of the fish fillet in the egg mixture, and then in the flour mixture.
3. **Place** a skillet over medium heat. Add the olive oil. When oil is hot, cook coated fillets on each side for 5 minutes, or until golden brown. Place fish fillets in plates. Serve with tartar sauce and steamed veggies.

LUNCH

1. Gluten-Free Cream of Mushroom Soup
Servings: 4-6
Serving size: 1 cup
Preparation time: 10 minutes
Cook time: 8 minutes
Ready in: 18 minutes

Nutrition Facts

Serving Size 156 g

Amount Per Serving

Calories 235 | Calories from Fat 183

	% Daily Value*
Total Fat 20.3g	**31%**
Saturated Fat 7.3g	**37%**
Trans Fat 0.0g	
Cholesterol 33mg	**11%**
Sodium 345mg	**14%**
Total Carbohydrates 11.8g	**4%**
Dietary Fiber 2.3g	**9%**
Sugars 1.3g	
Protein 3.6g	
Vitamin A 10%	Vitamin C 16%
Calcium 5%	Iron 16%

Nutrition Grade B

* Based on a 2000 calorie diet

Ingredients

- 8 ounces fresh mushrooms, sliced
- 1/4 cup shallots, chopped
- 1/2 cup cauliflower florets
- 1 tablespoon fresh thyme, chopped
- 1 bay leaf
- 2 cloves garlic, minced
- 3 tablespoons olive oil

- 4 tablespoons gluten-free corn flour dissolved in 4 tablespoons water
- 1 cup low-sodium chicken stock
- 1 cup light cream
- 1/2 teaspoon salt
- 1/4 teaspoon freshly ground black pepper

Directions

1. **Heat** olive oil in a 3 quart saucepan over medium heat. Add garlic and sauté until brown. Stir in the mushrooms, cauliflower, and shallots and cook for about 3 minutes.
2. **Pour** in dissolved corn flour and stir, about 2 minutes. Slowly pour the chicken stock. Add the thyme, bay leaf, and light cream; blend well until thick. Season with salt and pepper to taste.
3. **Ladle** soup into bowls and serve.

2. Hot Summer Chili

Servings: 6
Preparation time: 10 minutes
Cook time: 25 minutes
Ready in: 35 minutes

Nutrition Facts

Serving Size 254 g

Amount Per Serving

Calories 319	Calories from Fat 54
	% Daily Value*
Total Fat 6.0g	**9%**
Saturated Fat 0.9g	**5%**
Cholesterol 0mg	**0%**
Sodium 26mg	**1%**
Total Carbohydrates 53.0g	**18%**
Dietary Fiber 15.6g	**63%**
Sugars 6.3g	
Protein 16.7g	
Vitamin A 26%	Vitamin C 67%
Calcium 9%	Iron 33%

Nutrition Grade A

* Based on a 2000 calorie diet

Ingredients

- 2 tablespoons extra-virgin olive oil
- 2 large red onion, chopped
- 5 cloves garlic, crushed
- 2 tablespoons ground cayenne pepper
- 2 cups fresh tomatoes, chopped
- 1 cup black beans, drained
- 1 cup light kidney beans, drained
- 1 cup low-sodium chicken broth

- 1/2 cup green bell pepper, chopped
- 1/2 cup red bell pepper, chopped
- 1 cup corn kernels
- Salt and freshly ground black pepper, to taste
- 1/2 cup fresh cilantro, chopped

Directions

1. **Sauté** onion, garlic, and cayenne in a pot over medium heat for 5 minutes, or until onion is soft.
2. **Stir** in all the other ingredients, except for the cilantro, and bring to a boil. Reduce heat to low and simmer for 20 minutes or until vegetables are soft.
3. **Serve** topped with chopped fresh cilantro.

3. Salmon Egg Salad

Servings: 8
Serving size: 1 medium bowl
Preparation time: 10 minutes
Ready in: 10 minutes

Nutrition Facts

Serving Size 99 g

Amount Per Serving

Calories 185   Calories from Fat 109

% Daily Value*

Total Fat 12.1g	**19%**
Saturated Fat 2.5g	**13%**
Trans Fat 0.0g	
Cholesterol 168mg	**56%**
Sodium 66mg	**3%**
Total Carbohydrates 2.3g	**1%**
Dietary Fiber 0.9g	**4%**
Sugars 1.0g	
Protein 16.5g	
Vitamin A 6%	Vitamin C 3%
Calcium 3%	Iron 8%

Nutrition Grade B-

* Based on a 2000 calorie diet

Ingredients

- 14 ounces flaked salmon
- 1 medium red radish, diced
- 6 hard-boiled eggs, peeled and chopped
- 2 teaspoons chopped dill
- 1 1/2 teaspoons Dijon mustard
- 1/2-3/4 cup gluten-free mayonnaise
- 1/2 cup onion, chopped

- 1/2 teaspoon dried rosemary
- 1/2 sea salt
- 1/8 teaspoon black pepper
- 1/4 cup chives, chopped

Directions

Combine all ingredients in a large bowl; gently toss to coat. Chill for at least an hour and serve.

4. Fruity Chicken Salad

Servings: 8
Serving size: 1 medium bowl
Preparation time: 20 minutes
Ready in: 20 minutes

Nutrition Facts

Serving Size 176 g

Amount Per Serving

Calories 300	Calories from Fat 63

	% Daily Value*
Total Fat 7.0g	**11%**
Saturated Fat 1.1g	**5%**
Trans Fat 0.0g	
Cholesterol 65mg	**22%**
Sodium 68mg	**3%**
Total Carbohydrates 28.6g	**10%**
Dietary Fiber 3.1g	**12%**
Sugars 7.2g	
Protein 28.3g	
Vitamin A 2%	Vitamin C 36%
Calcium 4%	Iron 8%

Nutrition Grade B+

* Based on a 2000 calorie diet

Ingredients

- 1 1/2 pounds boneless chicken breast halves - cooked, cooled and cubed
- 1 cup oranges, drained
- 1 cup pineapple chunks, drained
- 2 cup gluten-free macaroni (cooked according to package instructions)
- 1/2 cup almonds, sliced
- 1 cup gluten-free light mayonnaise
- 2 teaspoons dried dill weed

- 2 teaspoons honey

Directions

1. **Stir** together the mayonnaise, dill weed, and honey in a small bowl.
2. **Combine** the chicken, macaroni, oranges, pineapple and almonds in a large mixing bowl. Pour dressing over chicken-fruit mixture and toss to coat. Chill in the fridge for at least 1 hour before serving.

5. BLT Salad
Servings: 8
Preparation time: 15 minutes
Cook time: 20 minutes
Ready in: 35 minutes

Nutrition Facts

Serving Size 172 g

Amount Per Serving

Calories 413 — Calories from Fat 307

% Daily Value*

Total Fat 34.1g	**53%**
Saturated Fat 10.8g	**54%**
Trans Fat 0.0g	
Cholesterol 46mg	**15%**
Sodium 1452mg	**61%**
Total Carbohydrates 8.5g	**3%**
Dietary Fiber 2.5g	**10%**
Sugars 5.2g	
Protein 21.8g	

Vitamin A 5% • Vitamin C 18%
Calcium 5% • Iron 12%

Nutrition Grade C-

*Based on a 2000 calorie diet

Ingredients

- 1 pound gluten-free bacon (recommended: Augason Farms, Hormel Foods, Range Brand)
- 3/4 cup gluten-free mayonnaise
- 1/4 cup low-fat milk
- 1 teaspoon garlic powder
- 1/8 teaspoon ground black pepper
- ¼ teaspoon salt

- 1 head romaine lettuce, shredded
- 2 large tomatoes, chopped
- 1 cup almonds, sliced

Directions

1. **Drizzle** skillet with olive oil and heat over medium high. Add bacon and cook until browned and crisp. Drain on paper towels. Crumble and set aside.
2. **Stir** together mayonnaise, milk, garlic powder, salt and black pepper in a small bowl until smooth.
3. **In a large salad bowl, mix** together the lettuce, tomatoes, bacon, and almonds. Pour dressing over bacon mixture. Toss well and serve.

6. Cedar Planked Salmon Fillets
Servings: 8
Preparation time: 30 minutes
Cook time: 20 minutes
Ready in: 50 minutes

Nutrition Facts

Serving Size 275 g

Amount Per Serving

Calories 572	Calories from Fat 331

	% Daily Value*
Total Fat 36.8g	**57%**
Saturated Fat 6.9g	**35%**
Cholesterol 143mg	**48%**
Sodium 822mg	**34%**
Total Carbohydrates 6.2g	**2%**
Dietary Fiber 1.4g	**6%**
Sugars 0.8g	
Protein 52.9g	
Vitamin A 10% • Vitamin C 28%	
Calcium 15% • Iron 23%	

Nutrition Grade B+

* Based on a 2000 calorie diet

Ingredients

- 2 (2 pound) salmon fillets, skin removed
- 1/3 cup gluten-free soy sauce
- 1/3 cup olive oil
- 1 1/2 tablespoons rice vinegar
- 1/4 cup green onions, chopped
- 1 teaspoon garlic, minced
- 1 tablespoon fresh ginger, grated
- 1 cup fresh dill, chopped

- ½ cup onions, chopped
- 1 fresh lemon, juiced

Directions

1. **Soak** 3 (12-inch) untreated cedar planks in warm water for at least 1 hour, but overnight would be even better.
2. **Place** the salmon fillets in a shallow dish. Mix together the soy sauce, olive oil, green onions, rice vinegar, garlic, and ginger in a small bowl. Rub the marinade into salmon fillets. Cover and marinate for 15-60 minutes.
3. **In a medium bowl, combine** dill, onions and lemon juice. Press mixture onto the top side of the fillets.
4. **Preheat** an outdoor grill for medium heat. Place the planks on the grill with the lid closed, for 3 minutes, or until they start to crackle and smoke.
5. **Place** the fillets carefully onto the planks, skin side down; spacing fillets 1 inch apart. Cover, and grill for about 20 minutes.
6. **Remove** planks from the grill. Place fillets onto plates and serve.

7. Chicken Fruit Spinach Salad

Servings: 4
Serving size: 1 medium plate
Preparation time: 1 hour and 20 minutes
Ready in: 1 hour and 20 minutes

Nutrition Facts

Serving Size 434 g

Amount Per Serving

Calories 610 — Calories from Fat 316

% Daily Value*

Total Fat 35.1g	**54%**
Saturated Fat 4.8g	**24%**
Trans Fat 0.0g	
Cholesterol 40mg	**13%**
Sodium 117mg	**5%**
Total Carbohydrates 59.4g	**20%**
Dietary Fiber 5.1g	**21%**
Sugars 51.4g	
Protein 21.7g	
Vitamin A 128%	Vitamin C 181%
Calcium 16%	Iron 22%

Nutrition Grade B

* Based on a 2000 calorie diet

Ingredients

- 1 1/2 cups cooked chicken, cut into bite-size pieces
- 8 ounces fresh spinach, torn into bite-size pieces
- 2 cups strawberries, hulled and sliced
- 2 cups mandarin orange segments
- 1/4 cup toasted walnuts, sliced

Dressing:

- 3 tablespoons sesame seeds
- 1/2 cup raw honey
- 1/2 cup olive oil
- 1/4 cup balsamic vinegar
- 1/4 teaspoon gluten-free Worcestershire sauce
- 1 medium onion, minced
- 1/2 tablespoon Dijon mustard
- salt and pepper, to taste

Directions

1. **Whisk** together all the dressing ingredients in a bowl. Cover and chill for one hour.
2. **In a large bowl, combine** the chicken, spinach, strawberries, orange, and walnuts.
3. **Pour** dressing over salad. Toss ingredients well to coat. Chill for 15 minutes then serve.

8. Thai Chicken Noodle Soup

Servings: 2-3
Serving size: 1 medium bowl
Preparation time: 10 minutes
Cook time: 18 minutes
Ready in: 28 minutes

Nutrition Facts

Serving Size 681 g

Amount Per Serving

Calories 394 — Calories from Fat 60

% Daily Value*

Total Fat 6.7g	**10%**
Saturated Fat 4.3g	**21%**
Trans Fat 0.0g	
Cholesterol 0mg	**0%**
Sodium 173mg	**7%**
Total Carbohydrates 73.3g	**24%**
Dietary Fiber 2.6g	**10%**
Sugars 5.7g	
Protein 11.8g	

Vitamin A 85% • Vitamin C 62%
Calcium 4% • Iron 14%

Nutrition Grade B-

* Based on a 2000 calorie diet

Ingredients

- 6 cups low-sodium chicken broth
- 1-2 fresh chicken breasts, chopped
- 1 stalk lemongrass, minced
- 1 bay leaf
- 1 tablespoon ginger, grated
- 1 large carrot, sliced
- 1 cup broccoli florets, trimmed

- 1 cup mushrooms, quartered
- 1/2 teaspoon. cayenne pepper
- 3 cloves garlic, minced
- 1/4 cup fresh lime juice
- 2 Tablespoon. gluten free soy sauce
- 1/4 cup coconut milk
- Salt and black pepper (to taste)
- a handful fresh cilantro, chopped
- 8-10 oz. gluten-free flat Thai rice noodles

Directions

1. **Boil** noodles according to package directions, or until al dente. Drain and set aside.
2. **Pour** chicken broth in a large pot and bring to a boil over high heat. Add chicken, broccoli, mushrooms, lemongrass, ginger, carrot, bay leaf. Turn heat to high and allow broth to boil for 1 minute. Cover the pot and reduce heat to medium. Simmer soup for 6 more minutes.
3. **While soup is simmering,** stir in cayenne, garlic, lime juice, and soy sauce. Turn heat to low and add the coconut milk; stir well.
4. **Place** cooked noodles into bowls. Pour soup over the noodles, then sprinkle with cilantro.

9. Gluten-Free Pepperoni Pizza

Servings: 6
Serving size: 2 pizza
Preparation time: 5 minutes
Cook time: 14 minutes
Ready in: 19 minutes

Nutrition Facts

Serving Size 368 g

Amount Per Serving

Calories 421	Calories from Fat 104
	% Daily Value*
Total Fat 11.5g	**18%**
Saturated Fat 3.1g	**15%**
Trans Fat 0.0g	
Cholesterol 162mg	**54%**
Sodium 2500mg	**104%**
Total Carbohydrates 13.8g	**5%**
Dietary Fiber 1.0g	**4%**
Sugars 2.4g	
Protein 57.0g	
Vitamin A 3%	Vitamin C 17%
Calcium 16%	Iron 15%

Nutrition Grade C

* Based on a 2000 calorie diet

Ingredients

- 1 (12-inch) Gluten Free refrigerated pizza crust dough (recommended: Bob's Red Mill, Pillsbury,)
- ¾ cup gluten-free pizza sauce
- 1 cup part-skim mozzarella cheese, shredded
- 30 slices gluten-free turkey pepperoni slices
- 2 medium tomatoes, diced
- 1/2 cup onion, chopped

Directions

1. **Preheat** oven to 400°F.
2. **Press** dough into a greased baking sheet.
3. **Bake** for 8 minutes. Remove dough from oven. Spread pizza sauce over dough. Add remaining ingredients on top. Return pizza into oven and bake for 6 to 9 minutes longer or until crusts are deep golden brown and cheese is melted. Divide into wedges and serve.

10. Quick N' Easy Gluten Free Chicken Stir Fry

Servings: 4-6 servings
Serving size: 1 medium bowl
Preparation time: 10 minutes
Cook time: 25 minutes
Ready in: 35 minutes

Nutrition Facts

Serving Size 252 g

Amount Per Serving

Calories 266	Calories from Fat 98

	% Daily Value*
Total Fat 10.9g	**17%**
Saturated Fat 2.6g	**13%**
Trans Fat 0.0g	
Cholesterol 101mg	**34%**
Sodium 178mg	**7%**
Total Carbohydrates 6.3g	**2%**
Dietary Fiber 1.4g	**6%**
Sugars 2.6g	
Protein 34.5g	
Vitamin A 39%	Vitamin C 49%
Calcium 4%	Iron 11%

Nutrition Grade B+

* Based on a 2000 calorie diet

Ingredients

- 1 tablespoon olive oil
- 1 1/2 pound boneless chicken breast cut into 1 inch cubes
- 2 cloves garlic, minced
- 1 small onion, chopped
- 1 cup mushrooms, sliced
- 2 cups broccoli, chopped
- 1 medium carrot, sliced

- 1/2 cup low-sodium chicken broth
- 3 tablespoon coconut aminos
- 1 teaspoon raw honey
- 1 teaspoon corn flour dissolved in 1 teaspoon water
- 1/4 teaspoon ground black pepper

Directions

1. **Heat** olive oil in a skillet over medium heat. Add the chicken, garlic, and onions; cook for 5 minutes or until chicken is golden brown. Stir in the mushrooms and cook for 10 minutes more.
2. **Add** broccoli, carrots, chicken broth and coconut aminos, and pepper.
3. **Cover** and simmer for 5 more minutes. Stir in corn flour and simmer until sauce thickens.

11. Easy Baked Tilapia

Servings: 4
Serving size: 1 fillet
Preparation time: 10 minutes
Cook time: 35 minutes
Ready in: 45 minutes

Nutrition Facts

Serving Size 158 g

Amount Per Serving

Calories 218	Calories from Fat 119
	% Daily Value*
Total Fat 13.3g	**20%**
Saturated Fat 6.5g	**32%**
Trans Fat 0.0g	
Cholesterol 78mg	**26%**
Sodium 115mg	**5%**
Total Carbohydrates 4.8g	**2%**
Dietary Fiber 0.6g	**2%**
Sugars 0.7g	
Protein 21.8g	
Vitamin A 7%	Vitamin C 19%
Calcium 3%	Iron 9%

Nutrition Grade D+

* Based on a 2000 calorie diet

Ingredients

- 1 pound tilapia fillets, about 4 fillets
- 3 tablespoons organic butter, melted
- 1 tablespoon olive oil
- 1 tablespoon fresh lemon juice
- 2 cloves garlic, minced
- 1 teaspoon Stevia
- 1/2 teaspoon pepper

- 1/2 teaspoon dried thyme
- 1 tablespoon parsley, chopped
- 1/3 cup gluten-free breadcrumbs
- 1 lemon, sliced

Directions

1. **Preheat** oven to 425. Grease a 9x13 inch baking dish lightly with olive oil.
2. **Rinse** fish filets and pat dry. Layer fillets in the prepared baking dish.
3. **Stir** together the garlic, butter, lemon juice, Stevia, thyme, parsley, and pepper in a small bowl. Pour and rub mixture over fish fillets; marinate for at least 15 minutes.
4. **Sprinkle** fillets with the breadcrumbs.
5. **Bake** for about 20 minutes or until fillets are flakey. Garnish with lemon slices.

12. Gluten-Free, Dairy-Free Cherry Turkey Lettuce Wraps

Servings: 4
Serving size: 2 turkey lettuce wraps
Preparation time: 10 minutes
Cook time: 16 minutes
Ready in: 26 minutes

Nutrition Facts

Serving Size 1778 g

Amount Per Serving

Calories 730	Calories from Fat 333

% Daily Value*

Total Fat 37.0g	**57%**
Saturated Fat 6.6g	**33%**
Trans Fat 0.0g	
Cholesterol 116mg	**39%**
Sodium 917mg	**38%**
Total Carbohydrates 62.3g	**21%**
Dietary Fiber 21.0g	**84%**
Sugars 33.5g	
Protein 48.0g	
Vitamin A 155%	Vitamin C 82%
Calcium 34%	Iron 52%

Nutrition Grade A

* Based on a 2000 calorie diet

Ingredients

- 4 tablespoons olive oil
- 1 1/2 cup yellow onion, diced
- 1 tablespoon garlic, minced
- 1 tablespoon ginger, minced
- 1 pound ground turkey
- 1/2 cup toasted almonds, sliced
- 1/2 cup fresh cilantro, chopped

- 2 tablespoons coconut aminos
- 1 teaspoon raw honey
- 1 teaspoon salt
- 1 teaspoon freshly ground black pepper
- 8 large iceberg lettuce leaves
- 1/2 cup dark sweet cherries, pitted and halved

Directions

1. **Heat** olive oil in a skillet over medium-high heat. Add the onions and garlic and sauté for about 5 minutes until lightly browned.
2. **Stir** in the turkey and cook for 8-10 minutes until the meat is no longer pink inside.
3. **Add** the almonds, cilantro, coconut aminos, and honey and cook for 3 minutes. Season with the salt and pepper.
4. **Fill** each lettuce leaf with a heaping spoonful of meat mixture and cherries.

13. Gluten Free Chicken Piccata

Servings: 4
Serving size: 1 chicken breast halved
Preparation time: 10 minutes
Cook time: 16 minutes
Ready in: 26 minutes

Nutrition Facts

Serving Size 242 g

Amount Per Serving

Calories 664 — Calories from Fat 446

	% Daily Value*
Total Fat 49.6g	**76%**
Saturated Fat 16.0g	**80%**
Trans Fat 0.0g	
Cholesterol 127mg	**42%**
Sodium 1187mg	**49%**
Total Carbohydrates 17.8g	**6%**
Dietary Fiber 4.0g	**16%**
Sugars 3.0g	
Protein 37.4g	

Vitamin A 19% • Vitamin C 22%
Calcium 14% • Iron 20%

Nutrition Grade B-

* Based on a 2000 calorie diet

Ingredients

- 4 boneless, skinless, organic, free-range chicken breast halves, pounded
- 1 cup ground almond meal
- 1/4 cup grated Parmesan cheese
- 1/2 teaspoon Dijon mustard
- 1 yellow onion, chopped
- 1 teaspoon sea salt
- 1/2 teaspoon freshly ground black pepper

- 4 tablespoons olive oil
- 4 tablespoons organic unsalted butter
- 1/2 cup organic gluten-free chicken broth
- 3 tablespoons lemon juice, freshly squeezed
- 2 tablespoons capers, rinsed
- 3 tablespoons organic butter
- 1/4 cup fresh parsley, chopped

Directions

1. **Combine** the almond meal, cheese, mustard, salt, and pepper together spread the mixture on a shallow dish.
2. **Rinse** the pounded chicken breasts in water and shake off the excess. Dredge the chicken in the flour mixture.
3. **Melt** 2 tablespoons butter in a large skillet over medium high heat; add the olive oil.
4. **Cook** chicken in butter and oil for approximately 3-4 minutes on each side until golden brown.
5. **Place** cooked chicken breasts on a serving dish and cover to keep warm.
6. **Stir** in the chicken broth, lemon juice and capers, scraping up any brown bits in the pan.
7. **Add** the chicken broth, lemon juice, and capers to the skillet; stirring and scraping up any brown bits in the skillet. Simmer until the sauce is reduced and reaches a light syrup consistency. Reduce heat to low and stir in remaining butter.
8. **Spoon** the sauce over the chicken breasts, top with chopped parsley. Serve with lemon slices or wedges.

14. Pork Tenderloin in Cranberry-Spinach Salad
Servings: 6
Preparation time: 20 minutes
Cook time: 20-25 minutes
Ready in: 40 minutes

Nutrition Facts

Serving Size 255 g

Amount Per Serving

Calories 351	Calories from Fat 152

	% Daily Value*
Total Fat 16.9g	**26%**
Saturated Fat 2.1g	**11%**
Trans Fat 0.0g	
Cholesterol 55mg	**18%**
Sodium 117mg	**5%**
Total Carbohydrates 26.8g	**9%**
Dietary Fiber 3.7g	**15%**
Sugars 19.1g	
Protein 25.4g	

Vitamin A 143%	Vitamin C 40%
Calcium 14%	Iron 28%

Nutrition Grade A

* Based on a 2000 calorie diet

Ingredients

- 1 pound pork tenderloin
- 1 cup cider vinegar
- 1 teaspoon Dijon mustard
- 1/4 cup raw honey
- 1 teaspoon dried thyme, crushed
- 3 tablespoons toasted sesame seeds
- 2 tablespoon raw honey

- 2 medium shallots, sliced
- 2 cloves garlic, crushed and chopped
- 1 cup dried cranberries
- 3/4 cup toasted pine nuts
- 1 pound baby spinach leaves, rinsed and torn into bite-size pieces

Directions

1. **Preheat** oven to 425 degrees F.
2. **Place** meat in shallow pan. Mix together cider vinegar, mustard, 1/4 cup honey and thyme in a bowl and brush the sauce mixture onto meat. Bake meat for 20-25 minutes. Slice meat into bite-size pieces and place into a large bowl.
3. **Whisk** together the sesame seeds, 2 tablespoons honey, shallots, garlic, 1/2 cup cider vinegar and olive oil and pour onto the meat. Add spinach, pine nuts and cranberries; toss well and serve.

15. Dijonnaise Tuna Salad on a Bed of Lettuce

Servings: 4
Serving size: 1 medium plate
Preparation time: 15 minutes
Ready in: 15 minutes

Nutrition Facts
Serving Size 202 g

Amount Per Serving

Calories 223	Calories from Fat 120
	% Daily Value*
Total Fat 13.3g	**20%**
Saturated Fat 1.5g	**7%**
Trans Fat 0.0g	
Cholesterol 17mg	**6%**
Sodium 181mg	**8%**
Total Carbohydrates 15.1g	**5%**
Dietary Fiber 5.9g	**24%**
Sugars 6.9g	
Protein 13.8g	
Vitamin A 4%	Vitamin C 19%
Calcium 2%	Iron 4%

Nutrition Grade A-

* Based on a 2000 calorie diet

Ingredients

- 1 (6 ounce) oil-packed tuna
- 1/2 cup gluten-free mayonnaise
- 1/4 cup walnuts, chopped
- 1 medium ripe avocado, sliced into chunks
- 1/4 cup scallions, minced
- 1 tablespoon Dijon mustard
- 1 medium onion, chopped

- 1 apple, cored and diced
- 4 leaves lettuce
- Sea salt and pepper to taste
- 1 teaspoon sweet pickle relish

Directions

1. **Whisk** together the mayonnaise, mustard, salt, and pepper in a medium bowl. Toss in tuna, onion, apple, walnuts, scallions and pickle relish. Cover and chill for 10 minutes.
2. **Line** the lettuce leaves on serving plates and fill the center with tuna mixture, then add avocado chunks on top.

DINNER

1. Gluten free Teriyaki Salmon
Servings: 4
Serving size: 1 (6 ounce) salmon steak
Preparation time: 15 minutes
Cook time: 10 minutes
Ready in: 25 minutes

Nutrition Facts

Serving Size 233 g

Amount Per Serving

Calories 408	Calories from Fat 213

	% Daily Value*
Total Fat 23.6g	**36%**
Saturated Fat 4.9g	**24%**
Cholesterol 107mg	**36%**
Sodium 113mg	**5%**
Total Carbohydrates 8.0g	**3%**
Dietary Fiber 0.9g	**4%**
Sugars 5.3g	
Protein 38.7g	
Vitamin A 4% •	Vitamin C 38%
Calcium 6% •	Iron 8%

Nutrition Grade B+

*Based on a 2000 calorie diet

Ingredients

- 4 (6 ounce) salmon steaks

Sauce:

- 1/4 cup gluten-free soy sauce (or coconut aminos)
- 1 teaspoon olive oil
- 1/2 cup lemon juice
- 1 tablespoon honey
- 1 tablespoon ginger, minced

- 1 teaspoon garlic, minced
- 1/2 cup spring onions, finely chopped
- 1/4 teaspoon ground black pepper
- 1 stalk lemongrass, minced
- 1 tablespoon sesame seeds

Directions

1. **Preheat** the oven to 180°C. Line a baking sheet with grease-proof or wax paper.
2. **In a small bowl, whisk** together the sauce ingredients.
3. **Place** the salmon into a large dish and pour the prepared sauce over the salmon and refrigerate for at least 30 minutes.
4. **Transfer** the salmon to the baking sheet and bake for 10-12 minutes or until cooked through. Serve with your choice of vegetable salad.

2. Honey Mustard Grilled Pork Chops

Servings: 8
Serving size: 1 pork chop
Preparation time: 10 minutes
Cook time: 6-8 minutes
Ready in: 16 minutes

Nutrition Facts

Serving Size 33 g

Amount Per Serving

Calories 169   Calories from Fat 64

	% Daily Value*
Total Fat 7.1g	11%
Saturated Fat 2.6g	13%
Trans Fat 0.0g	
Cholesterol 39mg	13%
Sodium 272mg	11%
Total Carbohydrates 12.8g	4%
Sugars 12.1g	
Protein 13.5g	

Vitamin A 0%	•	Vitamin C 5%
Calcium 2%	•	Iron 3%

Nutrition Grade F

*Based on a 2000 calorie diet

Ingredients

- 8 thin cut pork chops
- 1/3 cup raw honey
- 3 tablespoons lemon juice
- 1 teaspoon Frank's Red hot sauce
- 1 tablespoon apple cider vinegar
- 1 teaspoon gluten free Worcestershire sauce
- 2 teaspoons onion powder
- 1/4 teaspoon dried rosemary

- 3 tablespoons Dijon mustard
- 1 teaspoon cranberry juice

Directions

1. **Place** honey, lemon juice, hot sauce vinegar, cranberry juice, Worcestershire sauce, onion powder, rosemary, and mustard in a large re-sealable plastic bag.
2. **Place** pork chops in the plastic bag, tightly seal and gently shake to coat. Place bag in the refrigerator for at least 2 hours to marinate.
3. **Discard** marinade and grill pork chops over high heat for 6-8 minutes.

3. Beef Stuffed Cabbage

Servings: 6-8
Serving size: 1 beef stuffed cabbage
Preparation time: 15 minutes
Cook time: 1 hour and 15 minutes
Ready in: 1 hour and 30 minutes

Nutrition Facts

Serving Size 114 g

Amount Per Serving

Calories 201 — Calories from Fat 43

	% Daily Value*
Total Fat 4.7g	**7%**
Saturated Fat 1.6g	**8%**
Trans Fat 0.0g	
Cholesterol 74mg	**25%**
Sodium 73mg	**3%**
Total Carbohydrates 18.9g	**6%**
Dietary Fiber 0.6g	**2%**
Sugars 3.3g	
Protein 19.8g	

Vitamin A 1%	•	Vitamin C 7%
Calcium 1%	•	Iron 62%

Nutrition Grade B

* Based on a 2000 calorie diet

Ingredients

- 1 medium head cabbage
- 1 pound ground beef
- 1 cup cooked gluten free brown rice
- 1 organic, free-range egg
- 1 tablespoon dried parsley flakes
- 1/2 teaspoon garlic powder
- 2 celery stalks with leaves, finely chopped

- water to cover
- 1 1/2 cup gluten-free tomato sauce
- 1 tablespoon apple cider vinegar
- 1 tablespoon raw honey

Directions

1. **In a large pot over high heat, add** 2 quarts water and cabbage and bring to a boil for 15 minutes, or until outer leaves are tender. Drain cabbage and allow to cool completely. Using a paring knife, remove outer core of cabbage.
2. **Mix** together the beef, rice, egg, parsley flakes, garlic powder, and celery in a large bowl.
3. **Fill** the center of each cabbage leaf with 1/3 cup of the beef mixture. Fold sides over filling, tucking in the sides of the leaf.
4. **Pile up** the stuffed cabbage leaves in a large pot over medium low heat, placing the larger leaves on the bottom. Add the tomato sauce, vinegar, honey and enough water to cover. Simmer for about an hour, or until cabbage is very tender. Add tomato sauce as needed.

4. Raw Veggie Nuts and Seeds Salad

Servings: 8
Serving size:
Preparation time: 15 minutes
Cook time: 8-10 minutes
Ready in: 23 minutes

Nutrition Facts

Serving Size 221 g

Amount Per Serving

Calories 195 — Calories from Fat 113

	% Daily Value*
Total Fat 12.6g	**19%**
Saturated Fat 1.9g	**10%**
Trans Fat 0.0g	
Cholesterol 0mg	**0%**
Sodium 422mg	**18%**
Total Carbohydrates 16.3g	**5%**
Dietary Fiber 4.9g	**20%**
Sugars 5.5g	
Protein 7.3g	

Vitamin A 102%	•	Vitamin C 104%
Calcium 7%	•	Iron 16%

Nutrition Grade A

* Based on a 2000 calorie diet

Ingredients

- 3 medium carrots, diced
- 1/2 cup radish, diced
- 1 medium cucumber, diced
- 3 celery ribs,
- 1 head cauliflower
- 1 green bell pepper
- 1 red bell pepper

- 1 cup green cabbage
- 1 small onion
- 1/4 cup fresh basil
- salt and pepper
- 1/2 cup cashews, chopped
- 1/2 cup almonds, chopped
- 1/2 cup raw pumpkin seeds
- 1/2 cup raw sunflower seeds
- 1/2 tablespoon sea salt (or to taste)

Directions

1. **Toss** together all the vegetables in a large bowl.
2. **Heat** a skillet over medium heat. Dry roast the nuts and seeds until lightly browned and crisp. Season with salt and stir.
3. **Let cool,** and then toss the roasted nuts and seeds with the vegetables.
4. **Serve** with your choice of gluten-free salad dressing.

5. Parmigiano Beef Meatballs

Servings: 5
Serving size: 3 meatballs
Preparation time: 15 minutes
Cook time: 20 minutes
Ready in: 35 minutes

Nutrition Facts

Serving Size 233 g

Amount Per Serving

Calories 379　　　Calories from Fat 157

% Daily Value*

Total Fat 17.4g	**27%**
Saturated Fat 5.9g	**29%**
Trans Fat 0.0g	
Cholesterol 196mg	**65%**
Sodium 558mg	**23%**
Total Carbohydrates 6.5g	**2%**
Dietary Fiber 3.9g	**16%**
Sugars 1.6g	
Protein 49.5g	

Vitamin A 4%　　•　　Vitamin C 5%
Calcium 14%　　•　　Iron 147%

Nutrition Grade B

* Based on a 2000 calorie diet

Ingredients

- 1.5 pounds lean ground beef
- 3/4 cup gluten-free Parmigiano Reggiano, grated
- 1/2 cup flax meal
- 2 eggs
- 1/4 teaspoon garlic powder
- 1 medium onion, finely chopped
- 1 teaspoon sea salt

- 1/4 teaspoon freshly ground black pepper
- 1/2 cup warm water
- 1 cup gluten-free organic tomato sauce

Directions

1. **Preheat** oven to 350 degrees F.
2. **Mix** all meatball ingredients in a large bowl and shape into 2-inch meatballs. Arrange meatballs on a baking sheet, about 1 1/2-inches apart.
3. **Bake** for 20 minutes, or until internal temp reaches 160 degrees. Serve warm.

6. Grilled Rosemary Lime Swordfish

Servings: 4
Serving size: 1 swordfish steak
Preparation time: 1 hour and 10 minutes
Cook time: 10 minutes
Ready in: 1 hour 20 minutes

Nutrition Facts

Serving Size 169 g

Amount Per Serving

Calories 242	Calories from Fat 86

	% Daily Value*
Total Fat 9.5g	**15%**
Saturated Fat 2.1g	**11%**
Cholesterol 57mg	**19%**
Sodium 281mg	**12%**
Total Carbohydrates 3.7g	**1%**
Dietary Fiber 0.8g	**3%**
Sugars 0.6g	
Protein 29.2g	

Vitamin A 6%	Vitamin C 17%
Calcium 3%	Iron 11%

Nutrition Grade C+

* Based on a 2000 calorie diet

Ingredients

- 4 (4 ounce) swordfish steaks
- 2 teaspoons fresh rosemary, chopped (or 1 teaspoon dried rosemary)
- 3 cloves garlic, minced
- 1/2 cup white wine (or red wine vinegar)
- 1/4 teaspoon salt
- 1/4 teaspoon ground black pepper
- 2 tablespoon thinly sliced scallions
- 2 tablespoons lime juice

- 1 tablespoon finely chopped parsley
- 1 tablespoon olive oil
- 1 teaspoon dried thyme
- 4 slices lemon, for garnish

Directions

1. **Place** fish in a baking dish and season with salt and pepper. Combine garlic, 1 teaspoon rosemary, and white wine in a small bowl. Pour mixture over fish, turning to coat.
2. **Cover**, and place in fridge for at least 1 hour.
3. **In a small bowl, stir** together the scallions, lime juice, parsley, olive oil, thyme, and remaining rosemary.
4. **Preheat** grill for medium heat.
5. **Grill** fish for 10 minutes, turning once, or until fish is flakey. Place fish onto plates and pour the prepared lime sauce on top. Serve immediately.

7. Gluten-free Grilled Pineapple Burgers

Servings: 4
Serving size: 1 burger
Preparation time: 10 minutes
Cook time: 15 minutes
Ready in: 25 minutes

Nutrition Facts

Serving Size 401 g

Amount Per Serving

Calories 714　　　　Calories from Fat 215

　　　　　　　　　　　　　　% Daily Value*

Total Fat 23.9g	**37%**
Saturated Fat 10.8g	**54%**
Trans Fat 0.0g	
Cholesterol 228mg	**76%**
Sodium 551mg	**23%**
Total Carbohydrates 38.5g	**13%**
Dietary Fiber 4.4g	**18%**
Sugars 13.1g	
Protein 82.9g	
Vitamin A 8%	Vitamin C 36%
Calcium 30%	Iron 248%

Nutrition Grade B+

* Based on a 2000 calorie diet

Ingredients

- 2 pounds lean ground beef
- 1/2 cup gluten free teriyaki sauce
- 1 can (8 ounces) gluten free organic pineapple slices, juice reserved
- 4 lettuce leaves
- 4 slices Swiss cheese
- 4 slices tomato
- 4 gluten-free burger buns

Directions

1. **Mix** together beef and teriyaki sauce in a large bowl; season with salt and pepper.
2. **Divide** and form mixture into 4 patties, then drizzle each patty with the reserved pineapple juice. Place a pineapple slice on top of each patty.
3. **Discard** excess marinade. Grill the burgers over medium-low heat until cooked through.
4. **Layer** the burgers in the following order: top bun, lettuce, pineapple, cheese, burger patty, bottom bun.

8. Spinach N' Mushroom Stuffed Chicken
Servings: 4
Serving size: 1 stuffed chicken breast
Preparation time: 10 minutes
Cook time: 40 minutes
Ready in: 50 minutes

Nutrition Facts

Serving Size 186 g

Amount Per Serving

Calories 204 — Calories from Fat 104

	% Daily Value*
Total Fat 11.5g	**18%**
Saturated Fat 3.2g	**16%**
Cholesterol 68mg	**23%**
Sodium 530mg	**22%**
Total Carbohydrates 3.9g	**1%**
Dietary Fiber 1.3g	**5%**
Sugars 1.2g	
Protein 22.2g	

Vitamin A 56% • Vitamin C 19%
Calcium 3% • Iron 8%

Nutrition Grade C

* Based on a 2000 calorie diet

Ingredients

- 4 butterflied chicken breasts
- 1 cup button mushrooms, chopped
- 5 slices of nitrite and nitrate- free bacon
- 4-5 cups fresh spinach, chopped
- 1/2 teaspoon ground nutmeg
- 1 small onion, quartered
- 2 cloves garlic, minced
- Salt, to taste

- freshly ground black pepper, to taste
- Toothpicks

Directions

1. **Preheat** oven to 350 degrees F. Line a baking sheet with parchment paper.
2. **Place** a large skillet over medium-high heat. Add the bacon slices and cook each side until crispy. Place cooked bacon in a plate lined with paper towel and let cool.
3. **Cook** bacon in a large skillet over medium-high heat until crispy. Drain in paper towels and let cool.
4. **Leave** about 3 tablespoons of excess bacon fat in the pan and discard the rest.
5. **Add** mushrooms and garlic and sauté until vegetables are softened and lightly browned. Season with salt and pepper. Stir in the spinach, sprinkle with ground nutmeg. Cover the skillet and allow vegetables to simmer until the spinach has wilted. Add the cooked bacon and mix well. Remove the pan from heat. Spoon mixture into chicken breasts and secure with toothpicks.
6. **Place** stuffed chicken breasts on the prepared baking sheet. Bake for 18-20 minutes, or until chicken is no longer pink in the center.

9. Grilled Tilapia with Black Bean Mango Salsa

Servings: 2
Serving size: 1 tilapia fillet
Preparation time: 1 hour and 10 minutes
Cook time: 6-8 minutes
Ready in: 1 hour and 16 minutes

Nutrition Facts

Serving Size 220 g

Amount Per Serving

Calories 436   Calories from Fat 317

	% Daily Value*
Total Fat 35.2g	**54%**
Saturated Fat 5.5g	**28%**
Trans Fat 0.0g	
Cholesterol 83mg	**28%**
Sodium 645mg	**27%**
Total Carbohydrates 1.5g	**0%**
Protein 32.0g	
Vitamin A 4%	Vitamin C 11%
Calcium 4%	Iron 12%

Nutrition Grade D

*Based on a 2000 calorie diet

Ingredients

- 2 (6 ounce) tilapia fillets
- 1 clove garlic, minced
- 1 tablespoon dried parsley flakes
- 1 teaspoon dried basil
- 1 tablespoon lemon juice
- 1/3 cup extra-virgin olive oil
- 1 teaspoon ground black pepper
- 1/2 teaspoon salt

Salsa:

- 1/2 cup black beans, rinsed and drained
- 1 large ripe mango, peeled, pitted and diced
- 1 tablespoon freshly squeezed orange juice
- 2 tablespoons lemon juice, freshly squeezed
- 2 tablespoons red onion, minced
- 1/2 red bell pepper, diced
- 1 tablespoon fresh cilantro, chopped
- 1 teaspoon ground cumin
- 1/4 teaspoon sea salt, or to taste
- 1/4 teaspoon ground black pepper, or to taste

Directions

1. **In a mixing bowl, mix** all the salsa ingredients and refrigerate until serving.
2. **Place** tilapia fillets in a large dish.
3. **Whisk** together the garlic, parsley, basil, lemon juice, olive oil, salt, and pepper in a bowl. Pour marinade onto fillets and turn sides to coat. Place in the fridge for 1 hour.
4. **Preheat** a lightly oiled grill to medium-high.
5. **Discard** tilapia marinade and grill the fillets 3-4 minutes each side, or until flesh is opaque in the center, and flakes easily with a fork.
6. **Serve** the tilapia with mango salsa.

10. Grilled Lemon N' Lime Cod Fillets

Servings: 4
Serving size: 1 cod fillet
Preparation time: 20 minutes
Cook time: 8 minutes
Ready in: 28-30 minutes

Nutrition Facts

Serving Size 136 g

Amount Per Serving

Calories 184	Calories from Fat 73
	% Daily Value*
Total Fat 8.1g	**12%**
Saturated Fat 1.2g	**6%**
Cholesterol 62mg	**21%**
Sodium 558mg	**23%**
Total Carbohydrates 1.5g	**1%**
Dietary Fiber 0.7g	**3%**
Protein 26.1g	
Vitamin A 4%	Vitamin C 14%
Calcium 2%	Iron 4%

Nutrition Grade B

* Based on a 2000 calorie diet

Ingredients

- 1 pound cod, cut into 4 fillets (or other white fish)

Marinade:

- 2 tablespoons olive oil
- 1/4 cup fresh cilantro, chopped
- 1/2 teaspoon Stevia (or raw honey)
- 1 teaspoon sea salt
- 1/2 teaspoon black pepper

- 1/2 teaspoon cayenne pepper
- 1 tablespoon fresh lemon juice
- 1 tablespoon fresh lime juice
- 1 tablespoon lemon zest
- 1 tablespoon lime zest

Directions

1. **Place** fish in a large dish. Mix all ingredients for the marinade in a small bowl and pour over fish. Place in the fridge and marinate for 10-20 minutes.
2. **Preheat** a lightly oiled grill to medium-high.
3. **Grill** cod fillets for 4-6 minutes on each side, until golden brown.

11. Gluten-free Beef and Broccoli Stir-fry

Servings: 4
Serving size: 1 medium bowl
Preparation time: 35 minutes
Cook time: 10-15 minutes
Ready in: 45 minutes

Nutrition Facts

Serving Size 365 g

Amount Per Serving

Calories 423   Calories from Fat 140

	% Daily Value*
Total Fat 15.6g	**24%**
Saturated Fat 3.8g	**19%**
Trans Fat 0.0g	
Cholesterol 101mg	**34%**
Sodium 1845mg	**77%**
Total Carbohydrates 28.7g	**10%**
Dietary Fiber 3.2g	**13%**
Sugars 11.6g	
Protein 40.4g	
Vitamin A 58% • Vitamin C 140%	
Calcium 6% • Iron 124%	

Nutrition Grade A-

*Based on a 2000 calorie diet

Ingredients
Beef and Marinade:

- 1 pound beef flank steak, cut into strips
- 1/4 cup water
- 1/4 cup gluten-free soy sauce (or coconut aminos)
- 2 cloves garlic, minced
- 1/4 teaspoon ground pepper

Stir-Fry:

- 2 tablespoon olive oil
- 4 cups broccoli florets
- 1/2 cup onion, chopped
- 1/2 cup carrots, julienned

Sauce:

- 1 cup cold water
- 1/4 cup gluten-free soy sauce (or coconut aminos)
- 1/4 cup brown sugar
- 1 1/2 teaspoon ground ginger
- 1 teaspoon sesame oil
- 1/4 teaspoon red pepper flakes
- 1/4 cup cornstarch

Directions

1. **In a large bowl, whisk** together all the marinade ingredients. Add beef and marinate for 30 minutes.
2. **Heat** olive oil in a large pan or wok over medium-high heat. Stir in the beef and marinade, and cook for 3-5 minutes, or until meat is no longer pink.
3. **Add** onion and carrots, and fry for 2 minutes more; stirring often. Stir in the broccoli and fry for 1 more minute.
4. **Whisk** together all the sauce ingredients in a small bowl. Pour mixture over the beef and vegetable mixture, and cook for about 2-3 more minutes, or until sauce thickens.
5. **Serve** over hot brown rice.

12. Lemon and Herb Crusted Salmon Fillets

Servings: 4
Serving size: 1 salmon fillet
Preparation time: 10 minutes
Cook time: 10-15 minutes
Ready in: 20 minutes

Nutrition Facts

Serving Size 165 g

Amount Per Serving

Calories 249   Calories from Fat 111

	% Daily Value*
Total Fat 12.4g	**19%**
Saturated Fat 2.5g	**13%**
Trans Fat 0.0g	
Cholesterol 67mg	**22%**
Sodium 1283mg	**53%**
Total Carbohydrates 8.9g	**3%**
Dietary Fiber 1.0g	**4%**
Sugars 1.4g	
Protein 24.0g	

Vitamin A 6%	•	Vitamin C 27%
Calcium 5%	•	Iron 15%

Nutrition Grade C+

* Based on a 2000 calorie diet

Ingredients

- 4 (4-ounce) Atlantic Salmon Portions
- 2 teaspoons salt
- 1 teaspoon freshly ground black pepper
- 1 cup gluten-free breadcrumbs
- 2 tablespoons chives, finely chopped
- 2 tablespoons fresh thyme, finely chopped
- 2 tablespoons parsley, finely chopped

- 1 teaspoon Dijon mustard
- 1 teaspoon ginger, grated
- 1/2 teaspoon garlic powder
- 1/2 teaspoon onion powder
- 1 teaspoon lemon peel, grated
- 1/4 cup lemon juice

Directions

1. **Preheat** oven to 400 degrees F. Line a baking sheet with parchment paper.
2. **Season** both sides of salmon fillets with salt and pepper. Place skin side down on the prepared baking sheet.
3. **Combine** the breadcrumbs, chives, thyme, parsley, mustard, ginger, garlic powder, onion powder, and lemon peel in a medium bowl.
4. **Sprinkle** salmon with lemon juice and press the breadcrumb mixture on top of the salmon fillets.
5. **Cook** for 10-15 minutes, or until cooked through.

13. Spicy Almond Fish Sticks with Garlic Lime Tartar Sauce

Servings: 4
Preparation time: 45 minutes
Cook time: 10-15 minutes
Ready in: 55 minutes

Nutrition Facts

Serving Size 179 g

Amount Per Serving

Calories 604	Calories from Fat 503

	% Daily Value*
Total Fat 55.9g	86%
Saturated Fat 27.7g	139%
Trans Fat 0.0g	
Cholesterol 123mg	41%
Sodium 1372mg	57%
Total Carbohydrates 22.7g	8%
Dietary Fiber 1.9g	8%
Sugars 6.2g	
Protein 7.0g	

Vitamin A 11%	Vitamin C 8%
Calcium 3%	Iron 4%

Nutrition Grade F

* Based on a 2000 calorie diet

Ingredients

Fish sticks:

- 1 pound white fish, cut into 1x5-inch pieces
- 2 organic free-range eggs, whisked
- 1/2 cup blanched almond flour
- 1/2 teaspoon ground cayenne pepper
- 1/4 cup dried basil
- 3 cloves garlic, finely chopped

- 1 teaspoon salt
- 1/4 teaspoon freshly ground black pepper
- 1/2 cup coconut oil

Garlic Lime Tartar Sauce:

- 1 cup mayonnaise
- 1 teaspoon garlic powder
- 2 tablespoons lime juice
- 1 1/2 tablespoon dill pickle relish
- 1 tablespoon dried onion flakes
- 1/2 teaspoon salt

Directions

1. **Whisk** together all the ingredients for the tartar sauce until well-combined. Chill for at least 30 minutes until serving.
2. **Whisk** eggs in a medium bowl. In another bowl, combine almond flour, cayenne pepper, basil, garlic, salt, and pepper.
3. **Dip** fish sticks in egg, then flour mixture; coat well and place sticks in a plate.
4. **Heat** 1/4 cup coconut oil in a large skillet over medium high heat. Add half of the fish sticks and cook for 2-3 minutes on each side until well-browned. Leave enough room around fish sticks so that they aren't overcrowded.
5. **Drain** sticks on paper towels in a plate. Heat another 1/4 cup coconut oil and cook remaining half of the fish sticks. Serve with the prepared Garlic Lime Tartar Sauce.

14. Honey-Mustard Lemon Marinated Chicken
Servings: 4
Preparation time: 25 minutes
Cook time: 18-20 minutes
Ready in: 43 minutes

Nutrition Facts

Serving Size 154 g

Amount Per Serving

Calories 191 — Calories from Fat 70

% Daily Value*

Total Fat 7.8g	**12%**
Saturated Fat 0.9g	**4%**
Trans Fat 0.0g	
Cholesterol 73mg	**24%**
Sodium 472mg	**20%**
Total Carbohydrates 6.4g	**2%**
Dietary Fiber 2.9g	**12%**
Sugars 0.6g	
Protein 25.2g	
Vitamin A 14%	Vitamin C 21%
Calcium 7%	Iron 11%

Nutrition Grade A

* Based on a 2000 calorie diet

Ingredients

- 1 pound lean chicken breast, skinless and boneless
- 2 tablespoons Stevia
- 1/4 cup Dijon mustard
- 1 tablespoon olive oil
- 1/4 cup rosemary leaves, roughly chopped
- 1 lemon, zested and juiced
- 1 tablespoon cayenne pepper

- 1/2 teaspoon ground black pepper
- 1/2 teaspoon sea salt

Directions

1. **Place** chicken breasts in a 7 x 11 inch baking dish.
2. **Mix** together all ingredients except the chicken, in a medium bowl.
3. **Pour** prepared marinade over chicken; turn sides to coat. Cover, place in fridge, and marinate for 15 minutes to 1 hour, or overnight for best flavor.
4. **Bake** at 350°F for 18-20 minutes, or until internal temperature reaches 165°F. Pour extra sauce over top and serve.

15. Roasted Pork Tenderloin with Blueberry Sauce

Servings: 4
Preparation time: 10 minutes
Cook time: 35 minutes
Ready in: 45 minutes

Nutrition Facts

Serving Size 188 g

Amount Per Serving

Calories 218 Calories from Fat 54

% Daily Value*

Total Fat 6.0g **9%**
 Saturated Fat 1.6g **8%**
 Trans Fat 0.0g
Cholesterol 83mg **28%**
Sodium 300mg **13%**
Total Carbohydrates 9.2g **3%**
 Dietary Fiber 1.6g **6%**
 Sugars 5.9g
Protein 30.3g

Vitamin A 1% • Vitamin C 10%
Calcium 2% • Iron 10%

Nutrition Grade A-
* Based on a 2000 calorie diet

Ingredients

- 1/2 teaspoon dried basil
- 1/2 teaspoon dried rosemary, crushed
- 1/4 teaspoon garlic powder
- 1/4 teaspoon dry mustard powder
- 1/8 teaspoon celery seed
- 1/8 teaspoon dried parsley
- 1/8 teaspoon cayenne pepper

- 1/2 teaspoon sea salt
- 1/2 teaspoon freshly ground black pepper
- 1-1/4 pound pork tenderloin

Blueberry sauce:

- 1 small onion, diced
- 1-1/2 cups frozen blueberries, thawed
- 1/4 cup apple cider vinegar
- 1 teaspoon raw honey
- 1/2 teaspoon dried thyme
- 1/2 teaspoon freshly ground black pepper
- 1/2 tablespoon olive oil

Directions

1. **Preheat** oven to 400 degrees F. Place pork in a roasting pan.
2. **Combine** first 9 ingredients in a small bowl and rub onto the pork. Roast for 25 minutes (or until internal temperature reaches 155° F).
3. **In a small saucepan, sauté** onion in olive oil over medium-high heat, about 5 minutes. Add the remaining sauce ingredients and cook for another 5 minutes, or until sauce is thickened. Pool sauce on serving plates and top with slices of roasted pork.

DESSERTS and SNACKS

1. Carob Chip Cookies
Servings: 12
Serving size: 3 cookies
Preparation time: 10 minutes
Cook time: 8 minutes
Ready in: 18 minutes

Nutrition Facts

Serving Size 72 g

Amount Per Serving

Calories 234	Calories from Fat 124

% Daily Value*

Total Fat 13.8g	**21%**
Saturated Fat 1.8g	**9%**
Trans Fat 0.0g	
Cholesterol 36mg	**12%**
Sodium 123mg	**5%**
Total Carbohydrates 23.9g	**8%**
Dietary Fiber 1.4g	**6%**
Sugars 19.0g	
Protein 7.0g	

Vitamin A 1%	Vitamin C 0%
Calcium 8%	Iron 6%

Nutrition Grade D+

* Based on a 2000 calorie diet

Ingredients

- 3/4 cup raw honey
- 3/4 cup almond butter
- 2 1/4 cups almond flour
- 2 1/4 cups carob chocolate chips (chatfield's all natural carob chips)
- 1 teaspoon pure vanilla extract
- 1 teaspoon baking soda
- 1 teaspoon baking powder

- 1/2 teaspoon sea salt, or to taste
- 2 organic free-range eggs
- 1 teaspoon coconut oil (for greasing)

Directions

1. **Preheat** oven to 375 degrees F. Prepare a baking sheet and grease.
2. **In a medium bowl, mix** gradually the almond butter, honey, eggs and vanilla.
3. **In a different bowl, sift** the baking soda, gluten free flour mix, baking powder and salt. Mix in the butter mixture. Make sure to mix thoroughly. Finally, add the carob chips.
4. **Drop** cookie mixture on the baking sheet 2 inches apart using a teaspoon.
5. **Place** the baking sheet in the oven and bake for 8 minutes or until cookies turn to light brown.
6. **Let cool** for 2 minutes and remove cookies from the baking sheet.

2. Gluten Free Almond Butter and Banana Sandwiches

Servings: 8
Serving size: 1 sandwich
Preparation time: 15 minutes
Ready in: 15 minutes

Nutrition Facts

Serving Size 227 g

Amount Per Serving

Calories 477 — Calories from Fat 116

	% Daily Value*
Total Fat 12.9g	**20%**
Saturated Fat 6.8g	**34%**
Cholesterol 0mg	**0%**
Sodium 21mg	**1%**
Total Carbohydrates 86.3g	**29%**
Dietary Fiber 6.6g	**26%**
Sugars 42.3g	
Protein 4.8g	
Vitamin A 2%	Vitamin C 17%
Calcium 2%	Iron 3%

Nutrition Grade C

* Based on a 2000 calorie diet

Ingredients

- 1/4 cup coconut oil
- 1 cup almond nuts
- 10 drops liquid stevia (or raw honey)
- Pinch of salt, or to taste
- 16 gluten free sliced breads
- 8 ripe bananas, sliced lengthwise

Directions

1. **In a food processor, combine** coconut oil, almond nuts, stevia, and salt thoroughly until it forms a butter paste. Let cool.
2. **Spread** 2 tablespoons of almond butter on each pair of gluten free breads, add banana slices. Serve.

3. Citrus Berry Parfait
Servings: 5
Serving size: 1 parfait glass
Preparation time: 10 minutes
Ready in: 10 minutes

Nutrition Facts

Serving Size 104 g

Amount Per Serving

Calories 250	Calories from Fat 174
	% Daily Value*
Total Fat 19.3g	**30%**
Saturated Fat 4.7g	**23%**
Trans Fat 0.0g	
Cholesterol 0mg	**0%**
Sodium 1mg	**0%**
Total Carbohydrates 16.7g	**6%**
Dietary Fiber 6.1g	**24%**
Sugars 10.1g	
Protein 7.1g	
Vitamin A 2%	Vitamin C 22%
Calcium 3%	Iron 8%

Nutrition Grade B-

* Based on a 2000 calorie diet

Ingredients

- 1 cup coconut butter, melted
- 1/2 cup organic low-fat lemon yogurt
- 1 cup fresh blackberries or blueberries
- 1 cup fresh raspberries or strawberries
- 2 tablespoons raw honey
- 1 cup walnuts or almonds, chopped

Directions

1. **In a small bowl, mix together** honey, lemon yogurt, and coconut butter and stir thoroughly.
2. **In a separate bowl, combine** the blackberries and raspberries.
3. **Layer** the berries and coconut butter mixture in parfait glasses and sprinkle walnuts on top.

4. Gluten-Free Chocolate Cupcakes
Servings: 12
Serving size: 1 cup cake
Preparation time: 10 minutes
Cook time: 20 minutes
Ready in: 30 minutes

Nutrition Facts

Serving Size 71 g

Amount Per Serving

Calories 245	Calories from Fat 117

	% Daily Value*
Total Fat 13.0g	**20%**
Saturated Fat 1.4g	**7%**
Trans Fat 0.0g	
Cholesterol 36mg	**12%**
Sodium 75mg	**3%**
Total Carbohydrates 34.7g	**12%**
Dietary Fiber 1.3g	**5%**
Sugars 11.1g	
Protein 7.0g	

Vitamin A 1%	•	Vitamin C 0%
Calcium 8%	•	Iron 11%

Nutrition Grade D+

* Based on a 2000 calorie diet

Ingredients

- 130 grams almond butter
- 130 grams Gluten-Free Self-Rising Flour
- 130 grams Gluten-Free vanilla powder
- 1 ½ tablespoon carob powder
- ½ tablespoon pure vanilla extract
- 3 tablespoons raw honey
- 2 organic free-range eggs

Icing:

- 100 grams almond butter
- 100grams stevia

Directions

1. **Preheat** oven to 190 degrees C. Line paper liners in a standard cupcake tin (12 cupcakes).
2. **Whisk** together the honey and butter in a medium bowl until fluffy and pale. Add the eggs, carob powder, and flour and blend well.
3. **Place** the mixture in the cupcake tin with the paper liners and bake for 20 minutes.
4. **To prepare the icing,** mix together the stevia and butter in a bowl until soft and light. In a piping bag, place the mixture of the stevia and butter. Spoon the icing on top of each cupcake.

5. Garbanzo Bean Chocolate Cake

Servings: 12
Preparation time: 30 minutes
Cook time: 40 minutes
Ready in: 1 hour 10 minutes

Nutrition Facts

Serving Size 79 g

Amount Per Serving

Calories 280	Calories from Fat 85
	% Daily Value*
Total Fat 9.4g	**15%**
Saturated Fat 2.3g	**12%**
Trans Fat 0.0g	
Cholesterol 56mg	**19%**
Sodium 41mg	**2%**
Total Carbohydrates 38.5g	**13%**
Dietary Fiber 8.2g	**33%**
Sugars 14.2g	
Protein 12.0g	
Vitamin A 2%	Vitamin C 3%
Calcium 9%	Iron 19%

Nutrition Grade B-

* Based on a 2000 calorie diet

Ingredients

- 1 1/2 cups gluten-free semisweet chocolate chips
- 5 tablespoons almond butter
- 1 (19 ounce) can garbanzo beans, rinsed and drained
- 4 eggs
- 3/4 cup unrefined brown sugar
- 1/2 teaspoon baking powder
- 1 tablespoon unsweetened cocoa powder

- 1 teaspoon pure vanilla extract
- 1 tablespoon coconut oil

Directions

1. **Preheat** the oven to 350 degrees F (175 degrees C). Grease a 9-inch round cake pan with coconut oil.
2. **Place** the chocolate chips and almond butter into a microwave-safe bowl. Cook in the microwave for about 2 minutes, or until melted and smooth.
3. **Combine** the beans and eggs in the bowl of a food processor, and process until smooth. Mix in the sugar and the baking powder, melted chocolate mixture, and vanilla; blend until smooth and well blended. Transfer the batter to the prepared cake pan.
4. **Bake** for 40 minutes, or until a toothpick inserted into the center of the cake comes out clean or with only a few crumbs sticking to it. Cool in the pan on a wire rack for 10-15 minutes. Invert onto a serving plate and dust with cocoa powder. Serve.

6. Poached Pears and Vanilla Ice Cream with Chocolate-Mango Sauce

Serving: 8
Serving size: 1/2 poached pear
Preparation time: 15 minutes
Cook time: 16 minutes
Ready in: 31 minutes

Nutrition Facts

Serving Size 204 g

Amount Per Serving

Calories 239	Calories from Fat 57

	% Daily Value*
Total Fat 6.4g	**10%**
Saturated Fat 3.8g	**19%**
Cholesterol 8mg	**3%**
Sodium 23mg	**1%**
Total Carbohydrates 42.7g	**14%**
Dietary Fiber 4.2g	**17%**
Sugars 33.9g	
Protein 1.7g	

Vitamin A 2%	•	Vitamin C 8%
Calcium 5%	•	Iron 5%

Nutrition Grade D

* Based on a 2000 calorie diet

Ingredients

- 1 cup organic mango nectar
- 1 cup dry white wine
- 1/2 cup unrefined brown sugar
- 4 slightly under-ripe pears, peeled, halved, cored
- 4 ounces semisweet chocolate, chopped
- 1 cup gluten-free low-fat vanilla ice cream

Directions

1. **Mix** together the pear nectar, white wine and sugar in large saucepan and bring to a boil over medium-high heat.
2. **Add** pears and turn heat to medium-low. Simmer covered for 8 minutes, or until pears are tender.
3. **Using slotted spoon, transfer pear** halves to individual plates, cut side up.
4. **Turn** heat to medium-high. Boil poaching liquid for 8 minutes, or until syrupy and reduced by a quarter. Remove pan from heat. Whisk in chocolate until melted and sauce is smooth.
5. **Top** each pear half with 2 tablespoons vanilla ice cream and drizzle with warm chocolate sauce.

7. Almond-stuffed Baked Apples with Almond Whipped Cream
Servings: 6
Serving size: 1 stuffed apple
Preparation time: 20 minutes
Cook time: 20 minutes
Ready in: 40 minutes

Nutrition Facts

Serving Size 248 g

Amount Per Serving

Calories 231	Calories from Fat 53

	% Daily Value*
Total Fat 5.9g	**9%**
Saturated Fat 0.6g	**3%**
Trans Fat 0.0g	
Cholesterol 0mg	**0%**
Sodium 79mg	**3%**
Total Carbohydrates 40.5g	**13%**
Dietary Fiber 5.4g	**22%**
Sugars 31.9g	
Protein 7.4g	
Vitamin A 2%	Vitamin C 14%
Calcium 7%	Iron 4%

Nutrition Grade A

* Based on a 2000 calorie diet

Ingredients

- 6 apples
- 1/2 cup almond nuts, crushed
- 3 tablespoons raw honey
- 1/2 teaspoon nutmeg
- 1/4 teaspoon cinnamon
- Zest of 2 small lemons
- 2 tablespoons almond butter

- 1 pinch sea salt

Almond Whipped Cream:

- 1 1/2 cups gluten-free low fat whipping cream
- 1 teaspoon pure almond extract
- 1/2 teaspoon ground nutmeg
- 1 teaspoon ground cinnamon
- 1 tablespoon raw honey

Directions

1. **Preheat** oven to 375 degrees.
2. **Cut** out the cores of the apple with a paring knife and trim about 1/2-inch slice from the bottom of each apple.
3. **Place** cored apples in a baking dish and make them sit flat. Fill each apple with crushed almond nuts. Combine the honey, nutmeg, cinnamon, and lemon zest in a bowl and add to the stuffed apples.
4. **Stir** together almond butter and salt. Top each apple with 1 teaspoon of almond butter mixture.
5. **Bake** stuffed apples for 20–30 minutes. Transfer baked apples in serving plates.
6. **Combine** all the whipped cream ingredients in a blender or food processor and process until smooth and creamy.
7. **Spoon** 2 tablespoons of almond whipped cream on top of each stuffed apple.

8. Berry Medley Walnut Parfait with Coconut Vanilla Ice Cream
Servings: 6
Serving size: 1 parfait glass
Preparation time: 20 minutes
Ready in: 20 minutes

Nutrition Facts

Serving Size 238 g

Amount Per Serving

Calories 477   Calories from Fat 296

% Daily Value*

Total Fat 32.9g	**51%**
Saturated Fat 18.4g	**92%**
Cholesterol 5mg	**2%**
Sodium 24mg	**1%**
Total Carbohydrates 45.5g	**15%**
Dietary Fiber 6.0g	**24%**
Sugars 37.2g	
Protein 8.1g	
Vitamin A 2%	Vitamin C 62%
Calcium 6%	Iron 14%

Nutrition Grade C-

* Based on a 2000 calorie diet

Ingredients

- 1 1/2 cups fresh strawberries, sliced
- 1 cup fresh blueberries
- 1 cup fresh raspberries
- 1 lime, juiced
- 1 tablespoon raw honey
- 1 cup walnuts, chopped

Coconut Vanilla Ice Cream:

- 2 cups ice cold organic full-fat coconut milk
- 1/2 cup raw honey
- 2 teaspoons pure vanilla extract

Directions

1. **Prepare** the Coconut Vanilla Ice Cream: Combine coconut milk, honey, and vanilla in a blender. Cover and blend on High until smooth and frothy. Pour the liquid into a frozen ice cream bowl, cover, and start ice cream maker to churn it. Transfer to a freezer safe container; cover and serve.
2. **Chill** six parfait glasses.
3. **Toss** together the berries in a bowl and drizzle with honey and fresh lime juice.
4. **Layer** the berries, walnuts and coconut ice cream in parfait glasses.

www.ingramcontent.com/pod-product-compliance
Lightning Source LLC
Chambersburg PA
CBHW070907080526
44589CB00013B/1202